teach yourself®

the first world war

teach® yourself

the first world war
david evans

For UK order enquiries: please contact Bookpoint Ltd, 130 Milton Park, Abingdon, Oxon OX14 4SB. Telephone: +44 (0) 1235 827720. Fax: +44 (0) 1235 400454. Lines are open 09.00–18.00, Monday to Saturday, with a 24-hour message answering service. Details about our titles and how to order are available at www.teachyourself.co.uk

For USA order enquiries: please contact McGraw-Hill Customer Services, PO Box 545, Blacklick, OH 43004-0545, USA. Telephone: 1-800-722-4726. Fax: 1-614-755-5645.

For Canada order enquiries: please contact McGraw-Hill Ryerson Ltd, 300 Water St, Whitby, Ontario L1N 9B6, Canada. Telephone: 905 430 5000. Fax: 905 430 5020.

Long renowned as the authoritative source for self-guided learning – with more than 40 million copies sold worldwide – the **teach yourself** series includes over 300 titles in the fields of languages, crafts, hobbies, business, computing and education.

British Library Cataloguing in Publication Data: a catalogue record for this title is available from the British Library.

Library of Congress Catalog Card Number: on file.

First published in UK 2004 by Hodder Arnold, 338 Euston Road, London, NW1 3BH.

First published in US 2004 by Contemporary Books, a Division of the McGraw-Hill Companies, 1 Prudential Plaza, 130 East Randolph Street, Chicago, IL 60601 USA.

This edition published 2004.

The **teach yourself** name is a registered trade mark of Hodder Headline Ltd.

Typeset by Transet Limited, Coventry, England.
Printed in Great Britain for Hodder Arnold, a division of Hodder Headline, 338 Euston Road, London NW1 3BH, by Cox & Wyman Ltd, Reading, Berkshire.

Hodder Headline's policy is to use papers that are natural, renewable and recyclable products and made from wood grown in sustainable forests. The logging and manufacturing processes are expected to conform to the environmental regulations of the country of origin.

Impression number   10 9 8 7 6 5 4 3 2 1
Year   2010 2009 2008 2007 2006 2005 2004

contents

01

Europe in 1914 and the coming of war

This chapter will cover:
- the situation in Europe before the outbreak of war in 1914
- the nature of the relations between Europe's royal dynasties
- the reasons for the rivalry between the major powers and the stages by which Europe became divided into two armed camps
- crises and confrontations
- assassination at Sarajevo and the outbreak of war.

'Wherever I look … everything is restless and unsettled and everyone except ourselves is getting ready for war. This frightens me.'

(General Sir Henry Wilson in 1913)

Europe in 1914

A map of Europe in 1914 is very different from that of today. In the west, the frontiers of Portugal, Spain and France have remained much the same but in central and eastern Europe there have been significant changes. Germany was much larger then than it is today and Austria-Hungary, sometimes called the Habsburg Empire, dominated central Europe. Today, Austria and Hungary are two separate countries and the rest of that Empire is now a cluster of small independent states – the Czech Republic, Slovakia, Croatia and Bosnia. Present day countries such as Finland, Poland, Estonia, Latvia, Lithuania, Belarus and the Ukraine were then part of the vast Russian Empire but now

figure 1 Europe in 1914

they are all independent nations. At this time, although the struggle for home rule had begun, the whole of Ireland was part of Great Britain. The changes that have occurred since 1914 are the result of wars, revolutions and other political and social upheavals. No event contributed more to these changes than the First World War – the Great War of 1914–18.

The great European powers

Before 1914, Europe was dominated by five great powers – Britain, France, Germany, Austria-Hungary and Russia. Britain, major industrial nation and so-called 'workshop of the world' was also a great imperial power with an Empire that stretched across the world and over which, so it was claimed, 'the sun never set'. Her Empire provided her with raw materials for her industries and markets for her manufactured goods. The world's greatest fleet, the Royal Navy, guarded her important trade routes and it was a time when Britannia really did rule the waves! With such advantages Britain could stand aside from world events and concentrate on her own affairs and those of her Empire. During this time, often referred to as her period of 'splendid isolation', Britain faced numerous problems. In 1899, Britain became involved in a war in South Africa against the descendants of the early Dutch settlers, the Boers. To outsiders, the Boer War seemed a 'David and Goliath' affair and many regarded Britain as a colonial tyrant. Some European countries, particularly Germany, were sympathetic to the Boers and the German Kaiser went as far as to hint that he might help the Boers in their conflict with Britain. During the same period, Britain very nearly went to war with France over quite a trivial issue – the ownership of a small town in the Sudan called Fashoda.

France, another great imperial power, also faced major difficulties. In 1870, she was tricked into a war with her neighbour, Prussia, and the Franco-Prussian War ended in her humiliating defeat. Afterwards, she had to pay the costs of the war and surrender the provinces of Alsace and Lorraine to Prussia. Even worse, the Prussian chancellor, Otto von Bismarck, used the occasion to declare the birth of a German Empire and Wilhelm I was proclaimed first Kaiser of the new Empire that embraced nearly all the German-speaking states in central Europe. In France, these events nearly led to a revolution and the French people voted to become a republic, the Third Republic. Their disgraced emperor, Napoleon III, and his family were forced to spend their last years living in exile in England. Humbled and embittered, the French looked for a chance to avenge their humiliation and regain their lost provinces.

It is often not appreciated that Germany did not exist as a nation until 1871. The creation of a united Germany was virtually the work of one man, Bismarck, nicknamed the 'Iron Chancellor'. In 1888, Frederick III who was married to Victoria, daughter of Queen Victoria, the Queen of Britain, succeeded his father but he reigned for less then four months before he died of throat cancer. The German throne next passed to Kaiser Wilhelm II, soon to be infamously known as 'Kaiser Bill' who quickly rid himself of the restraining influence of Bismarck, and began to follow reckless policies that were to endanger the peace of Europe.

The Emperor Franz Ferdinand, already in his mid-sixties, ruled over the ramshackle multi-racial empire of Austria-Hungary. Famed for his austere living – it is said that his spartan bedroom only contained a bed and washstand – his life was dogged by a series of unusual personal tragedies. His brother, the self-appointed Emperor of Mexico, was executed by rebels whilst his son, Rudolf, shot himself as part of a suicide pact with his mistress at Mayerling. In addition, his wife, the Empress Elizabeth, was stabbed to death by an anarchist whilst another son, Karl Ludwig, died from typhoid after drinking the waters of the River Jordan whilst on a pilgrimage. By this time, the heir to the throne of Austria-Hungary was his remaining closest relative, his nephew, Franz Ferdinand and it was the assassination of this nephew that was to lead directly to the outbreak of war in 1914.

Tsar Nicholas II who ruled the massive Russian Empire that stretched from Europe across Asia to the Pacific Ocean in the east also faced difficulties. Dominated by his German-born wife and influenced by a self-styled holy man, the evil Rasputin, a tragedy of his life was that his only son, Alexei, was a haemophiliac. Nicholas's autocratic rule was under threat from revolutionary groups who sought to overthrow the monarchy and introduce a democratic style of government and bring about other much needed reforms. In 1904, Nicholas foolishly tried to gain popularity by becoming involved in a war against small and presumably weak Japan, as he thought he could gain an easy victory. However, it was a folly and the Russians were defeated and humiliated on land and sea. This led to even greater unrest amongst the Russian people and an attempted revolution. Faced by strikes and demonstrations, order was restored when Nicholas offered a range of concessions to the Russian people including an elected assembly. Even so, the situation in Russia remained fraught with danger.

The feuding royal dynasties

Apart from republican France, royal families ruled the major powers of Europe. The leading royal dynasties were the British House of Hanover, the German House of Hohenzollern, the Russian House of Romanov, the long established House of Habsburg in Austria-Hungary and in Italy, the House of Savoy. Although intermarriage had created close ties of kinship, it in no way prevented the royal families from feuding.

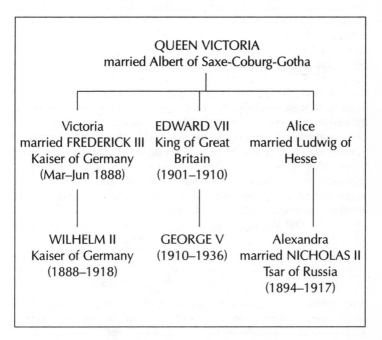

figure 2 the feuding royal houses

Of the nine children of Queen Victoria, the Queen of Britain, the eldest, Princess Victoria, married the German Kaiser, Frederick III, popularly known as Fritz. In 1859, she gave birth to a son, Wilhelm who, as Wilhelm II, became Kaiser in 1888 and was to rule Germany during the First World War. Victoria's second child, Edward, a portly high-living prince, succeeded his mother to the throne in 1901 and reigned until his death in 1910 when he was succeeded by his son, George V. Alice, Victoria's third child, married the German prince Louis of Hesse. Their daughter, Alexandra, married Nicholas II, Tsar of Russia. This meant that the British King, George V, was a cousin of both the German Kaiser, Wilhelm II, and Alexandra, the Tsarina of Russia. Since their mothers were Danish princesses and sisters, George V was also a cousin of Nicholas II and although they got on well, neither liked nor trusted their German cousin, Wilhelm II. It is interesting to note that in 1901, her son, King Edward VII, her grandson, Kaiser Wilhelm, and Tsar Nicholas II of Russia all attended Queen Victoria's funeral. Yet within 20 years, two would themselves be dead and the third facing self-imposed exile.

Great power rivalry

Each of the great powers was ambitious, mindful of its own needs and jealous of the others. As the years passed this jealousy turned first to bitter rivalry. Frenchmen looked forward to what they considered would be an inevitable war with Germany during which they would gain revenge for their defeat in 1870 and which would give them the chance to regain Alsace and Lorraine. For his part, the German Kaiser was jealous of Britain's colonial expansion and commercial prosperity and wanted to extend his own country's influence in the world. He was convinced that the future greatness of Germany was dependent on her becoming a naval power. As he put it, 'We have fought for a place in the sun and won it. Our future is on the water.' Naturally the British became alarmed when Germany seemed intent on challenging her long-standing supremacy on the seas.

The scene changed dramatically in 1906 when the British launched the first of a new class of powerful, ironclad warships. Called HMS *Dreadnought*, its range, speed and firepower outclassed German battleships and made them obsolete. The Germans referred to their own battleships as being *fünf-minuten* ships, 'five-minute ships', the time they would last when confronted by a *Dreadnought*. During the years that followed, Britain and Germany became involved in a naval race to build the greatest number of *Dreadnought*-class battleships. As

figure 3 the Balkans in 1914

Admiral von Tirpitz masterminded the building of a powerful German fleet, so the British government dithered as to the number they should build. The British public had no such doubts. A popular British music-hall song of the day was 'We want eight and we won't wait'. The effects of this rivalry were serious; the building of such ships proved a great financial burden for both countries.

Austria-Hungary and Russia had long been rivals in an area of south-east Europe known as the Balkans. The whole region had once been part of the Ottoman Empire and had been ruled by the Turks. As the Turkish Empire fell apart, so both powers tried to take advantage of the situation and extend their influence in the area. Both had common frontiers with the former Turkish provinces whilst Russia claimed the additional advantage of sharing the same Slav heritage as many of the Balkan peoples.

In the squabble between the two countries, Kaiser Wilhelm firmly backed Austria-Hungary. Germany had also tried to get on good terms with the Sultan of Turkey by building a railway that linked Berlin with Baghdad and promising financial and military aid. Neither Austria-Hungary nor Russia seemed to appreciate that the peoples of the Balkans hoped to set up their own independent Slav state free from their influence. One Balkan country more than any other stood firmly against Austrian domination – little Serbia.

From rivalries to alliances and ententes

Alliances are formed when nations bind themselves together by treaties and this often happens when countries share a common fear and look for security on the basis of safety in numbers. During the years when Bismarck was the Chancellor of Germany, he planned a series of alliances with other countries that were intended to safeguard Germany from any possible threat from Russia or the chance that France might wage a war of revenge. In 1879, he formed a Dual Alliance with neighbouring Austria-Hungary by which the countries agreed to help each other if attacked by another. The Dual Alliance became a Triple Alliance when they were joined by Italy who was, at best, a half-hearted member. Although the Kaiser claimed that the Triple Alliance was defensive in nature, the existence of such a powerful bloc of nations in central Europe spread alarm amongst their neighbours. Since both France and Russia thought the Triple Alliance was aimed at them, it was inevitable that they would come together to gain greater security and this they did in 1894. The threat posed by Kaiser Wilhelm's Germany also made it necessary for Britain and France to settle their differences. Many hatchets had to be buried before the two countries could reach a closer understanding and in 1904, an Anglo-French Entente was agreed. It became popularly known as the Entente Cordiale. An entente is not a formal alliance but more an agreement to settle differences and work more closely together. Eventually a Triple Entente was formed that embraced France, Britain and Russia. It was now the Kaiser's turn to be alarmed since it appeared that the Entente powers encircled Germany. More significantly, the creation of a system of alliances and ententes meant that the European great powers were now divided into two hostile armed camps, clearly posing a threat to the future peace in Europe.

figure 4 Europe divided – the Triple Alliance and the Triple Entente

In such a situation all that was needed was a provocative act, a spark, to plunge Europe into war. The German Kaiser, described as having 'the touchiness of a prima donna and the conceit of a small child', was not best suited to dealing with such a situation.

'Now tell us all about the war,
And what we fought each other for.'

(Robert Southey, 1774–1843)

The coming of war

A crisis is a decisive moment, a turning point when at a time of danger, things can go either one way or the other. There were two areas in Europe where provocative acts led to crises which might have led to war – Morocco in North Africa and the Balkans.

In 1905, Kaiser Wilhelm II challenged French rights to be involved in the affairs of Morocco when he travelled to Tangier to pay a courtesy call on the Sultan. During his visit he made a provocative speech openly supporting Moroccan independence and challenging the right of France to exercise authority over the country. The French were outraged by the Kaiser's audacity and the following year the major European powers attended a conference at the Spanish port of Algeciras to discuss the issue. If Wilhelm's aim was to test the solidarity of the Triple Entente, he would have been disappointed since Britain and Russia stood firmly behind France. The outcome was an unwelcome rebuff for the German Kaiser but the issue of Morocco was far from settled. In 1911, tribesmen attacked the Moroccan town of Fez and the French sent troops to restore order and garrison the town. The German response was to dispatch the gunboat *Panther* to the nearby port of Agadir on the pretext of safeguarding their country's interests in the area. This was a rash act of brinkmanship. Once again Britain stood by France and even went as far as to begin the partial mobilization of the Royal Navy! Not wishing to risk war, the Kaiser was forced to

THE BOILING POINT.

A *Punch* cartoon of 1912 which shows the leaders of the great European powers sitting on a pot marked 'Balkan troubles', indicates their concern as the situation in the region reaches boiling point.

back down. Wilhelm had once again lost face and the affront angered the German people who put the blame squarely on Britain. Britain was now seen as the main enemy and a wave of anti-British feeling swept Germany. The years that followed were the most frantic in the naval race between the two countries and with the Kaiser angry and frustrated, he was likely to act even more irresponsibly than before.

In 1898, Bismarck commented, 'If there is ever another war in Europe, it will come out of some dammed silly thing in the Balkans'. How true his prophecy turned out to be. In 1908, Austria-Hungary annexed Bosnia. It was an act that infuriated Bosnia's neighbours and unsettled the whole Balkan region.

During the year 1912, the Balkans was torn by unrest that ended in war. The First Balkan War of 1912 lasted barely 50 days and the following year this was followed by the Second Balkan War. The outcome of the wars led to much bitterness and was to decide which side the various Balkan states would join in the event of any future war.

Assassination at Sarajevo

At around 11 a.m. on the morning of Sunday 28 June 1914, the heir to the throne of Austria-Hungary and his wife were assassinated by a teenage student in Sarajevo, the capital of Bosnia. Bosnia, forcibly annexed by the Austrians in 1908, was a dangerous country for any member of the Austrian royal house to visit. The state visit by the heir to the Austrian throne was a provocative act and always likely to attract a response from one of the secret societies that were part of the Pan Slav movement. The victims were Archduke Franz Ferdinand and his wife Sophie. As we have seen, the Archduke became heir to the throne as the result of the number of bizarre tragedies that befell the Emperor's family. He was said to have been 'a humourless, hectoring man, who killed animals in large numbers, but was conscientious and not unintelligent'. He was certainly a devoted family man. He married Sophie, who came from an aristocratic but poor Czech family, against the wishes of the Emperor. The marriage was declared morganatic which meant that any children would be debarred from succeeding to the throne. The assassin, Gavrilo Princip, had three accomplices. They were Serbians who belonged to Union or Death, a secret society better known as the Black Hand.

The Archduke arrived in the Bosnian capital fully aware of the risks he was taking. It was also his wedding anniversary. Together with his wife, he proceeded from the railway station to the town hall in a procession of open cars. On the way, a bomb was thrown at their car but it fell on the folded roof and bounced under the car following behind. Even though 20 people were wounded, the Archduke did not lose his composure. Sadly, his good fortune did not survive their return journey. His driver lost his way and as he stopped to reverse the car, Princip ran from the crowd of onlookers and fired at his victims from point-blank range. The stricken Archduke cried out to his wife, 'Sophie, Sophie don't die. Live for our children.' The Duchess died first followed by the Archduke, his jugular vein severed by a bullet. No murder in history has had such calamitous consequences.

'War by timetable'

The sequence of events that followed the assassination of Archduke Franz Ferdinand seemed to follow a prescribed order and has been described by the historian A. J. P. Taylor as 'War by timetable'. He wrote, 'Sarajevo had set in motion machinery which could not be stopped' (*War By Timetable*, 1969).

Even though an investigation by Austrian officials failed to find any link to connect the Serbian government with the murders, the matter was not allowed to rest. In the Austrian capital, Vienna, there were politicians and military leaders who urged war and saw the assassination as a heaven-sent opportunity to eliminate Serbia, who was regarded as the champion of Pan Slavism in the Balkans.

Crucial to the outcome was the attitude of Germany, Austria-Hungary's powerful ally. In the event, the Kaiser let it be known that Germany would 'stand faithfully by Austria-Hungary, as required by the obligations of their treaty'. In effect, the guaranteed backing of Germany gave the Austrians carte-blanche, complete freedom of action, to do as they wished. They sent an ultimatum to Serbia listing ten demands. The Serbs reply was conciliatory and they rejected only one demand that appeared to infringe their country's sovereignty. As Austria-Hungary began to mobilize her forces for war so Britain and France called for a conference to discuss the crisis. On 28 July 1914, Austria invaded Serbia. Although the Tsar's confidante,

Rasputin, warned, 'Let papa not plan war, for with the war will come an end of Russia and yourselves', Nicholas's reaction was to put his own forces on a war footing. When a German demand for an end to these preparations was ignored, Germany declared war on Russia. Next the Germans sought an undertaking of neutrality from France. The French government replied that it would be 'guided by her own interests' and began to mobilize for war. On 3 August 1914, the Germans falsely claimed that French aircraft had dropped bombs on a German city and declared war on France.

The British involvement

Although Britain was a member of the Triple Entente, she was not committed to joining the war. At home, public opinion was divided. One view was expressed by a newspaper that commented 'We care as little for Belgrade (the capital of Serbia) as Belgrade cares for Manchester' but others thought that, as a matter of honour, Britain should immediately side with her Entente partners. But in the end the matter was settled for them. Years before the war, the Germans had devised a plan, the Schlieffen Plan, that was intended to bring about the speedy defeat of France and avoid the possibility of having to fight on two fronts. In order to be able to outflank the French armies, the plan required the Belgian government to agree to the passage of German troops across their country. When the request was turned down, German troops invaded Belgium. Years before in 1839, Britain and other European powers including Germany had agreed to a treaty by which they collectively guaranteed the neutrality of Belgium. The British government sent an ultimatum to Germany demanding the withdrawal of their troops and that the neutrality of Belgium be respected. The Kaiser ignored the demands after being advised that Britain would be unlikely to go to war 'just for a scrap of paper'. When, on 4 August 1914, the time set for a response to the ultimatum expired, Britain declared war on Germany. As the last minutes of peace ticked away, the British foreign secretary, Sir Edward Grey, standing in the window of his office in Whitehall likened what was happening in Europe to the actions of a man in the street below who was dimming the gaslights. He famously remarked, 'The lamps are going out all over Europe; we shall not see them lit again in our lifetime.'

NO THOROUGHFARE

BRAVO, BELGIUM!

A *Punch* cartoon of August 1914 shows plucky Belgium standing firm against German threats.

What became of the assassins?

Immediately after he had fired the shots that killed Franz Ferdinand, Gavrilo Princip attempted to commit suicide. He failed and was dragged to the local police station. Under torture, he betrayed the names of his accomplices and they were arrested. Their trial lasted a month and at the end all but Princip were sentenced to death. The actual assassin was under age and escaped the hangman's noose by just a fortnight. Instead he was sentenced to spend 20 years in an Austrian prison. The Austrian authorities did not intend him to live and he died in April 1918 with one arm amputated and suffering from tubercular ulcers.

Prior to his execution, one of Princip's accomplices, Nedeljiko Cabrinivic, wrote a letter to his three-year-old daughter:

'My child, the only thing that your father can leave you is his honest and untarnished name ... When you grow up and you will hear about those tumultuous times in which your father lived. If you understand them, you will forgive him ... Be honest and love the people whose roots are your own.'

To the Slav people, the assassins were heroes. Later, a museum was built in Sarajevo to commemorate Princip's bravery and was named in his honour.

02

the opening moves on the Western Front

This chapter will cover:

- the initial reaction to the outbreak of war
- the Schlieffen Plan
- the importance of the retreat from Mons and the Battle of the Marne
- the Christmas truce of 1914.

'Tramp, tramp, the grim road from Mons to Wipers
I've 'ammered out this ditty with me bruised and bleedin' feet.
Tramp, tramp, the dim road – we didn't 'ave no pipers,
And bellies that was 'oller was the drums we 'ad to beat.'

(*The Red Retreat, Rhymes of a Red Cross Man*,
Robert Service, 1916)

Reactions to the outbreak of war

Press reports and rumour meant that the last weeks of peace had something of an unreal quality. There was no mood of impending crisis and people continued with their everyday lives and enjoyed their summer pleasures. In Germany, the Kaiser left for a yachting holiday in the Norwegian fjords; in France, the President made plans to visit Russia; in Britain, the King opened a conference on the issue of home rule for Ireland. However, once war was declared, governments found it easy to stir up patriotic fervour. Jubilant crowds in jingoistic mood took to the streets in Berlin, Paris, Vienna, St. Petersburg and London to cheer and sing. In Britain, military leaders spoke of a war that would be 'over by Christmas'. In Berlin, the German Chancellor remarked solemnly, 'Just for a scrap of paper, Great Britain is going to make war with a kindred nation that desires nothing better than to be friends with her.' Whilst the Kaiser reflected, 'To think that George and Nicky have played me false! If my grandmother [Queen Victoria] had been alive, she would never have allowed it', his son, the Crown Prince took a different line and claimed to be delighted at the prospect of 'a gay and jolly little war'. He further jested that it would be a case of 'lunch in Paris, dinner in St. Petersburg'. In towns and cities across Europe, men queued to 'join up' for what they regarded as the start of a great adventure. They might have better considered the words of a wise American president, 'Older men declare war. But it is the young that must fight and die.'

Opening moves and the Schlieffen Plan

As nations continued to mobilize their armies and fleets, Germany had already worked out a master plan for the quick and decisive defeat of her enemies. The German military leaders had long feared the prospect of engaging two enemies simultaneously – Russia in the east and France in the west.

Count Alfred von Schlieffen, the former German Chief of Staff, calculated that it would take Russia longer to mobilize her forces than France and therefore decided to use the bulk of the German army to win a speedy and decisive victory over the French. France defeated, he would then turn to the east and deal with the Tsar's armies. His plan, the 'revolving door technique', required the German armies to sweep through neutral Belgium into northern France and advance to the west of Paris. The Germans would then swing south in a wide arc to outflank the French armies defending their common border with Germany and force them to surrender. If the Belgians resisted, the main obstacles to the German advance would be Liege and Namur since these fortress towns would be stoutly defended. The plan also involved risks – the Russians might mobilize more quickly than expected and the invasion of Belgium might draw Britain into the war. Schlieffen, who died in 1912, did not live long enough to see his plan put into effect. On 4 August 1914, German troops invaded Belgium and within a fortnight Brussels had fallen and Antwerp was under siege. Meanwhile a British Expeditionary Force (BEF), under the command of Field Marshal Sir John French, had sailed for France. Once landed, it took up position next to the French in the path of the advancing Germans.

Mons and the Marne

The BEF was made up of some 70,000 regular soldiers and reservists. Referred to scathingly by the German Kaiser as 'a contemptible little army', they were highly trained infantrymen and what they lacked in numbers they more than made up for in their professionalism and skilled use of their main weapon, the Lee-Enfield rifle.

The first British encounter with the enemy occurred close to the Belgian coal-mining town of Mons when Irish Dragoons came face to face with a force of Uhlans, German cavalry. At Mons, the BEF fought the Germans to a standstill among the slag heaps close to the Mons-Conde Canal and the battle gave birth to the legend of the 'Angels of Mons' when some British soldiers claimed to have been helped by angel-like English archers from a bygone age. The rumour was repeated by returning wounded soldiers who were probably delirious but it was nevertheless believed by some. The early British success at Mons was short lived. To the south the French were in retreat and this meant that the BEF risked being outflanked. They had no choice other than to retreat. The historian John Terraine has written, 'Mons scarcely rates as a battle at all, there was certainly no evidence that it slowed the Germans to any noticeable extent' (*Mons*, 1960).

The retreat from Mons was a slow rearguard action doggedly fought by exhausted and footsore British infantrymen described by Terraine as 'men stumbling more like ghosts than living soldiers, unconscious of everything about them, but still moving under the magic impulse of discipline and regimental pride'. At Le Cateau, British units under Major General Smith Dorrien stood to fight the Germans who were in hot pursuit and there they briefly held overwhelming forces. Fighting from shallow, hastily prepared trenches, both the Germans and the British inflicted and suffered heavy losses before continuing their retreat. Afterwards, the British commander-in-chief, Field Marshal Sir John French, showed his resentment at Smith Dorrien's decision to stand and fight by removing him from command on the pretext of bad health. Heavily outnumbered, the BEF aimed to delay the German advance long enough for the French to regroup and rush forward fresh reserves. After only ten days of fighting, the Germans were still surging forward and closing in on Paris. Only one obstacle lay in the way – the River Marne.

Although the speed of the German advance had been impressive, it had created problems. As they advanced, so their lines of communication became stretched and with the Russians mobilizing more speedily than expected, troops had to be withdrawn and sent to the east. At this point, the German High Command decided to tinker with Schlieffen's original plan. Instead of sweeping to the west of Paris and encircling the French capital, they decided to pursue the retreating French to the east of the city. This proved to be a major blunder. The move weakened the left flank of the German army and gave the Allies, the name now given to those fighting on the side of France and Britain, the chance to counterattack. In Paris, the governor of the city assembled reserves and sent them forward to the front line in taxis, the famous 'taxis of the Marne'. For two weeks, the Battle of the Marne raged along a 250-kilometre (155-mile) front. As the German position became increasingly precarious, so they were forced to retreat from the River Marne to a new defensive line to the north-east along the River Aisne. The outcome of the battle has been referred to as 'the miracle of the Marne' and because of its significance, some have gone as far as to regard it as 'the most important of the twentieth century'. It halted the German advance, ensured the failure of the Schlieffen Plan and brought about the dismissal of senior German generals. It is only possible to speculate on what the effect a German victory might have had on the outcome of war and even the future history of Europe. What was certain was that any chance of a quick end to the war had finally gone and the war would definitely not be over by Christmas!

The 'race to the sea' and the Ypres salient

The Germans next turned their attention to the flat coastal region of Flanders – the northern border area between Belgium and France – and here each side struggled to outflank the other as they tried to reach the coast in what became known as the 'race to the sea'. The German aim was to extend their front line to the Channel coast and gain control of the strategically important ports of Dunkirk, Calais and Boulogne. All now depended on the ability of the British and Belgians to hold on to the coastal strip around the River Yser and, inland, the city of Ypres.

The battle that followed, the First Battle of Ypres, was the last major battle fought on the Western Front in 1914. It lasted a month and, helped by the arrival of French reinforcements and flooding of a stretch of the coastal region, the Germans failed to break through. During the battle, British casualties totalled nearly 60,000, the majority being original members of the BEF It was but a taste of things to come since Ypres, or 'Wipers' as British soldiers called it, was to witness further bloody encounters and even greater loss of life.

The German failures on the Marne and at Ypres led to a position of stalemate as each side tried, but failed, to dislodge the other. The nature of the warfare was such that soldiers could only find safety by 'digging in' and it was at this stage of the war that the construction of trenches began in earnest. Soon a continuous network of trenches stretched the 800 kilometres (497 miles) from the English Channel to the Swiss border.

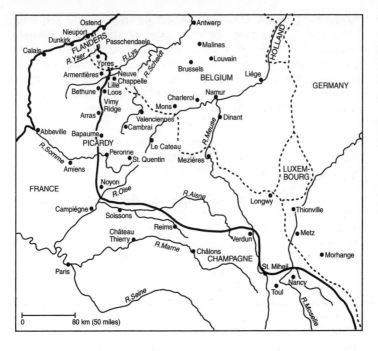

figure 5 the Western Front – the front line at the end of 1914

The Christmas truce of 1914 – did it really happen?

Christmas Day 1914 witnessed one of the most notable and unusual events of the First World War. An unofficial truce occurred along sections of the Ypres battlefield during which British and German troops openly fraternized in the land between the opposed trenches, no man's land. It began during a lull in the fighting on Christmas Eve when, after dark, the Germans lit up a Christmas tree and began to sing carols before men on both sides climbed over the top of their trenches, shook hands and wished each other 'a merry Christmas'. They exchanged gifts of cigarettes and cigars as well as souvenirs such as cap badges and family photographs and some even exchanged addresses so that they could make contact after the war. On Boxing Day, a football match was arranged and photographs taken. The truce, which was not general and only took place in sections of the lines, involved hundreds of soldiers and gave both sides the opportunity to bury their dead. The event, described as 'an oasis of sanity in a deadlocked war', gave rise to concern in both the British and German High Commands since they saw it as a threat to the fighting spirit of their troops. They took steps to ensure that the episode would never be repeated.

One explanation of this unusual event is that earlier in the year the Pope had proposed a Christmas Day truce and many of the German soldiers involved came from Bavaria, a largely Roman Catholic area of Germany. It is possible that the unofficial truce came about as an attempt to implement the Pope's wishes.

03

stalemate and a widening war

This chapter will cover:
- the situation on the Western Front during 1915
- the involvement of Turkey and Italy in the war
- the war on other fronts
- the fate of Germany's colonies.

'When all is said and done, the war was mainly a matter of holes and ditches.'

(*Memoirs of an Infantry Officer*,
Siegfried Sassoon, 1930)

The situation at the start of 1915

Although the First World War (1914–18) never became truly a world war to the extent of the Second World War (1939–45), its military operations did extend widely across several fronts in Europe and beyond into the Middle East, Africa and even the Pacific. This was brought about because other powers such as Turkey, Italy and Japan became involved in the conflict and also because Britain, France and Germany had overseas possessions that bordered on each other.

It should also be remembered that imperial powers such as Britain, France and Germany soon involved their colonies in the conflict. In the case of Britain, this meant that Australia, New Zealand, Canada, India and South Africa came to the assistance of their 'Mother Country'. In order to exploit Britain's dependency on imported foods and raw materials and hinder the passage of imperial forces to Europe, German surface raiders ranged across the Atlantic, Indian and Pacific Oceans tracking down and sinking British merchant ships and troopships. Meanwhile on the Western Front the stalemate continued.

The Western Front during 1915

During 1915, Allied and German generals set out to break the deadlock on the Western Front no matter what the cost. The first major offensive came when British troops tried to recapture the village of Neuve Chapelle that the Germans had occupied at the end of the previous year. Although the British were successful in their objective, the battle highlighted two important issues – it revealed the first signs of a shortage of shells and it also provided the first evidence of the human cost of launching frontal attacks against an enemy holding well-prepared defensive positions. The Germans were surprised by the tactic used by the British, which presented them with a target of a solid wall of khaki men, side-by-side and even more so by the fact that once one line had been mowed down by machine-gun fire, another appeared. The lesson was not learned by the British and a same familiar pattern was to be followed time and time again with dire consequences. In the spring came the Second Battle of Ypres, chiefly remembered for the first use of chemical warfare in the form of chlorine gas. The first victims were French colonial troops who panicked, threw away their weapons and fled, then two days later gas was used against the Canadians at St. Julian. Since it was known that ammonia present in urine had the effect of minimizing the effects of chlorine gas, and with no respirators available at this stage of the war, the best the Canadians could do was tie pieces of cloth soaked in urine over their mouths and nostrils. Imagine how awful this was – although there was much worse to come!

During the battle little ground was yielded to the Germans but at a cost – 60,000 casualties. In the autumn, British and French forces combined to launch another offensive along the River Aisne and although the Germans were driven back, they regained the lost ground in a series of counterattacks. During the offensive, French casualties totalled 120,000, British, 50,000 and German, 165,000. In spite of the carnage, once again nothing was achieved but it did lead to the dismissal of the British commander-in-chief, Field Marshal Sir John French.

New nations involved

The outcome of the Second Balkan War decided the nature of the expansion of the war in the Balkans. With Serbia supported by the Allies, because of the earlier Balkan wars, it was inevitable that Bulgaria would join the Central Powers, the name applied to Germany and her allies. In 1916 Romania joined Britain and France, to be followed by Greece in 1917, but even more significant was the entry of Turkey into the war.

Although generally regarded as a nation in decline, Turkey was in a position to blockade the Dardanelles and control entry into the Black Sea and she was also strategically placed to threaten Egypt and the Suez Canal. Before the war, both Britain and Germany had gone to great lengths to win the friendship of Turkey. Sixty years earlier, at the time of the Crimean War, Britain and France had fought to defend Turkish interests against her traditional enemy, Russia, but now Britain and France were allies of Russia, and Turkey faced a conflict of loyalties. Within the Turkish government, factions supported both sides but most influential was the pro-German nationalist,

Enver Pasha, who had once been employed in the Turkish embassy in Berlin. Whilst the Germans had built the Berlin to Baghdad railway and sent their officers to help train and modernize the Turkish army, the British had agreed to build two *Dreadnought*-type battleships for the Turkish government and these were nearing completion in British shipyards. At the start of the war, Winston Churchill, the First Lord of the Admiralty, ordered the seizure of the two ships and this outraged the Turks who accused the British of bad faith and treachery. The matter was finally decided when two German battleships, the *Goeben* and the *Breslau*, outran British warships in the Mediterranean Sea to reach Constantinople and once there, the Germans generously offered them to Turkey to compensate for 'England's theft'. The Turks next closed the Dardanelles to Allied shipping, an act that effectively blockaded Russia since it prevented shipments of armaments reaching her Black Sea ports. Within a week Britain, France and Russia declared war on Turkey. The first Turkish move was to invade the neighbouring Russian province, the Caucasus, with the intention of threatening the Baku oilfields but their troops, unprepared for the harsh winter conditions, were routed. However, as we shall discover, Turkey still had an important part to play in the war.

Since Italy still distrusted France and had no quarrel with Germany, Italian opinion was divided about the war and it was only after much diplomatic manoeuvring that Italy abandoned her membership of the Triple Alliance and joined the Allies. Italy had long coveted regions along her borders with Austria-Hungary and Italian nationalists saw involvement in the war as a means of acquiring those territories. In 1915, Italy agreed the Treaty of London with the Allies. At the time, the terms of the treaty were kept secret but they included a promise that, after the war, Italy would gain the south Tyrol, Trieste, Istria and a part of the Dalmatian coast. It was also agreed that Albania, just across the Adriatic Sea, would become an independent Muslim state with Italy responsible for her foreign policy. In May of that year Italy finally declared war on Austria-Hungary but it would be another year before she finally entered the war against Germany. From an Allied point of view, Italian entry into the war would provide them with important bases for their Mediterranean operations and at the same time, open up a new front that would divert Austro-Hungarian resources from the Eastern Front where Austria-Hungary was fighting Russia. Clearly Italy was tempted into the war on the side of the Allies by promises of a share of the spoils once victory was won but to Britain and France her involvement in the war soon proved to be more a liability than an asset. With her soldiers inadequately trained, lacking in fighting qualities, inadequately supplied with munitions and other war materials and, General Cardona apart, led by officers of poor quality, Italy was far from prepared for war.

The war on other fronts

The involvement of Turkey and Italy added a new dimension to the war. In addition to the Western and Eastern Fronts, the armies of the Allies and the Central Powers now faced each other in Serbia and Salonika, on the Italian Front and along Turkey's common border with Russia. To these would soon be added a campaign on the Turkish mainland, in Palestine, Mesopotamia and against German colonies in east and south-west Africa.

figure 6 military operations in Europe during 1915

figure 7 Serbia finally overrun

Although isolated from her Allies, Serbia caused problems for Austria-Hungary and at the start, the Austrian offensive against Serbia turned into a humiliating failure and was easily repulsed. Although poorly equipped, the Serbs fought well and by the end of 1914 were able to launch their own offensive and expelled the invaders from their country. Enough was enough and the Germans sent Field Marshal August von Mackensen to sort things out and organize a combined Austrian, German, Bulgarian offensive against troublesome Serbia. With Austro-Hungarian forces crossing the River Danube and advancing from the north and west and the Bulgarians moving from the east in an outflanking movement, the Serbs had no choice but to retreat westward. Led by a hero of earlier years, the wily, 67-year-old Radomir Putnik, the Serbs avoided encirclement by making their way across the mountains of Albania in most appalling weather conditions to reach the Adriatic Coast and there some 150,000 were taken on board Allied ships and transferred to the island of Corfu. Meanwhile, to the south a British and French force had landed in Salonika to help 'plucky little Serbia' but with their attempt to advance northwards blocked by the Bulgarians, they had no choice other than to dig in. Isolated and involved in little action, they became nicknamed the 'Gardeners of Salonika'.

After declaring war, the Italians attempted a series of offensives against the Austrians in the Alps and along the River Isonzo in the general direction of Trieste. Warfare in the Alps was always destined to be hard going and require special skills and powers of endurance and the severe weather and hazardous conditions soon blighted the initial enthusiasm of the Italians. The struggle to win control of the high ground and mountain ridges ended in stalemate and both sides were forced to dig in along the Isonzo.

The fate of Germany's colonies

In accordance with her alliance with Britain and with the hope of expanding her territories in the Pacific, Japan declared war on Germany in 1914. The Japanese were quick to occupy Germany's island possessions – the Palau, Caroline, Marianas and Marshall Islands and also besieged and captured Tsingtao, a port on the Chinese mainland that had been leased by Germany. Also during 1914, New Zealand took possession of Samoa whilst Australian troops occupied Papua and New Guinea.

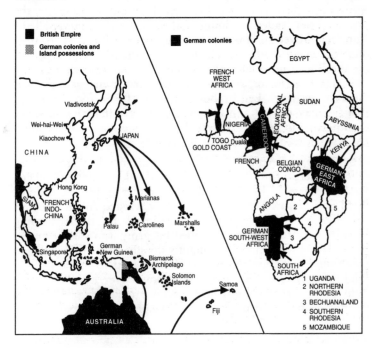

figure 8 Germany's colonies in the Pacific and Africa

During the nineteenth century, Germany had taken part in the stampede to colonize Africa, the so-called 'scramble for Africa'. By 1914, German colonies in Africa included Togo, the Cameroons, German South-West Africa (present day Namibia) and German East Africa (present day Tanzania) and all were adjacent to British and French colonies. At the start of the war, Togo was overrun by British and French forces during a three-week campaign and by the end of the year, the Cameroons had also been taken following a jungle campaign involving British, French and Belgian troops. German South-West Africa, which lay next to British South Africa, presented more of a problem. In South Africa, memories of the Boer War were still fresh and the cause of much animosity and many former Boers, now known as Afrikaners, remembered with great bitterness that the British had burned down their homesteads, rounded up their women and children and interned them in concentration camps where thousands had died of disease and malnutrition. Now they looked for the opportunity to avenge these atrocities by supporting Germany. In 1914, a rebellion broke out led by the former Boer leader, Solomon Maritz. The rebels attracted the support of over 10,000 men but after some initial success, their efforts came to nothing. Fortunately, for the Allies, the majority of the Boers, including their former generals Louis Botha and Jan Smuts, were prepared to join their former enemy in the war against Germany. Led by Botha, South African forces invaded the German colony and in spite of the fact that thousands of South African soldiers deserted to the Germans, loyal South Africans forced the colony to surrender.

The Allies experienced the greatest resistance in German East Africa where a force largely made up of Askaris, native soldiers, and commanded by the formidable soldier of genius, Colonel Paul von Lettow-Vorbeck, successfully resisted Allied attempts to invade the colony. However, faced by overwhelming numbers, Lettow-Vorbeck divided his army into small units of irregulars and during a brilliantly fought guerrilla campaign continued to harass the Allies. He managed to evade capture and his irregulars managed to hold down over 130,000 British and Empire troops until he finally surrendered in 1918 – a fortnight after an armistice had been signed in Europe.

04

the Eastern Front

This chapter will cover:
- Russia's entry into the war
- the nature of the war on the Eastern Front
- the successes of Hindenburg and Ludendorff
- the reasons for the Russian failures on the Eastern Front.

'... very shaken, part of it altogether smashed and the rest falling back.'

(A Russian officer's view of his army in 1915)

Russia's involvement in the war

Russia entered the war with the same enthusiasm shown by the other major powers, and as part of an effort to rally popular support for the Tsar, a large crowd outside the Winter Palace cheered Nicholas. Amongst his first actions was to change the name of his capital city from the German-sounding St. Petersburg to the more acceptable Russian version, Petrograd and in an effort to prove her loyalty, Alexandra, the Tsarina who was German by birth, became involved in hospital work. At the start of the war, the Tsar wanted to assume command of the Russian armies himself but he was prevailed upon to appoint his uncle, the Grand Duke Nicholas Nicholaievich. The Grand Duke, the nephew of a former tsar Alexander II, was unusually tall and full of energy, he was also a good administrator but a man of only limited experience as a military commander. Even so, as a soldier and strategist he was far superior to the generals who served him. The Russian Minister for War was Vladimir Sukhomlinov, a devious man who was flattered to win favours and was both corrupt and inefficient. Jealous of Grand Duke Nicholas who despised him, Sukhomlinov was to be more responsible than any other for the disasters that lay ahead.

The Eastern Front

The Eastern or Russian Front stretched from the Baltic Sea southward across East Prussia and the Russian province of Poland to Galicia in Austria-Hungary and along this front, the armies of Tsar Nicholas II confronted those of Austria-Hungary and Germany. The Germans, who had placed great emphasis on winning a speedy victory against France in the west, hoped that the Austro-Hungarians would be able to hold a defensive line and counter any Russian moves in the east with minimum German involvement. Unfortunately these hopes were dashed by the failure of the Schlieffen Plan and the unexpected speed with which the Russians mobilized their armies. On the face of it the Russians had one major advantage – they possessed near limitless manpower resources. The Russian regular army's pre-war strength was 1.4 million to which mobilization added a further 3.1 million and behind these lay umpteen millions of peasants willing to join the ranks and die for 'Mother Russia'. With the capacity to overrun their enemy by sheer weight of numbers, it was not surprising that it was known as the 'steamroller army'. Against this, the Russian armies were badly equipped and lacked modern weapons and whilst they did reasonably well against the Austro-Hungarians, they fared badly against the Germans who showed the value of their superior military training and modern weaponry. Unlike the Russians, the Germans were also able to benefit from a modern railway network that allowed them to move their troops speedily from one battlefront to another. In addition, they also had the advantage of being forewarned of their enemy's movements since they were able to intercept uncoded messages sent by the Russians on their radio transmitters. During the winter months, the harsh conditions on the Eastern Front would prove to be exceptionally demanding for the men of both sides.

The opening campaigns

It was in response to an urgent appeal from France to relieve pressure brought by the German onslaught in 1914 that the Russians launched their first offensive into East Prussia. There, Generals Paul von Rennenkampf, a Russian in spite of his German-sounding name, and Alexander Samsonov won an unexpected victory that caused the Germans some immediate concern. The German response was to transfer units from the Western Front and send Generals Paul von Hindenburg and Erich Ludendorff to take charge of their armies and sort things out. Hindenburg came from a Prussian landowning family that could trace its aristocratic and military traditions back to the thirteenth century, he was a veteran of many campaigns and during the Franco-Prussian War had been awarded the Iron Cross. It was said that he won promotion 'by ordinary process, not brilliance', and unlike most officers of his rank lacked both influence and money. He retired from the army in 1911 but was recalled in 1914 at the age of 67. Erich Ludendorff was a man of far more modest origins. Son of an impoverished landowner, he was commissioned into one of the less fashionable regiments. Nearly 20 years Hindenburg's junior, he was ambitious, a man of great mental and physical energy and of the two, he was the

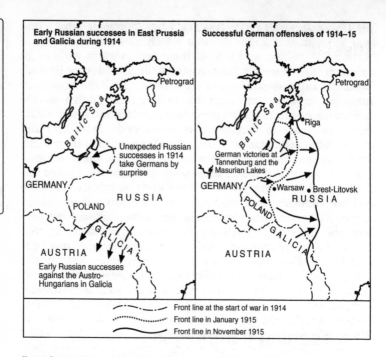

figure 9 campaigns on the Eastern Front during 1914 and 1915

true military genius. As the war progressed, the aged Hindenburg and dynamic Ludendorff, 'twinned by their triumphs in East Prussia', gradually emerged as the real power in Germany in both military and political affairs.

With the two Russian armies separated by the Masurian Lakes, Ludendorff decided to concentrate on the one advancing from the south and at the Battle of Tannenburg, the Germans won a resounding victory and took 90,000 prisoners. Afterwards, the disgraced Samsonov took his own life. During the following month, the Germans turned their attention to the second Russian army and at the Battle of the Masurian Lakes they were again victorious. This time, the Russians lost some 120,000 casualties and were forced to retreat in disorder and so the legend of the invincibility of Hindenburg and Ludendorff was born.

1915 – A year of mixed fortunes for Russia

Although the Russians had suffered at the hands of the Germans, they continued to make progress against the Austrians and in the spring of 1915 were able to fight their way across the Carpathian Mountains and advance towards the River Danube before shortages of supplies and ammunition brought their advance to an abrupt halt. Within the German High Command there was some disagreement as to whether greater emphasis should be given to the Eastern or Western Front. Some, such as General Erich von Falkenhayn, favoured an offensive in the west but Hindenburg wanted to press home their advantage in the east and force Russia out of the war. In the end the views of the more influential Hindenburg prevailed. Strengthened by the arrival of reinforcements from the west, the Germans launched an offensive that took the Russians by surprise. First, their defences were shattered by a massive bombardment during which 700,000 shells were fired in four hours and then with the Germans advancing along the whole front, the Russians found themselves facing the risk of being caught in a pincer movement between the Austrian armies now advancing from Galicia in the south and German armies advancing from East Prussia in the north. The Russians had no other choice than to retreat and this allowed the Germans to advance rapidly and capture Warsaw first and then Brest-Litovsk. A Russian general reported to the Tsar '…a third of the men have no rifles. These poor devils have to wait patiently until their comrades fall so they can pick up their weapons. The army is drowning in it's own blood'. Driven from Poland, the Russians retreated further eastward so that they were now fighting on their own soil. Although the Russians fought bravely enough and resisted strongly, the Germans were able to advance nearly 500 kilometres (311 miles) before the Grand Duke's armies were able to establish a new defensive line that extended from Riga on the Baltic Sea to Romania in the Balkans. It was soon to become 'six hundred miles of mud and horror' along which Russian casualties stood at 2 million with a further million lost as prisoners. The suffering of the soldiers was horrendous, yet disastrous as the whole episode may have been, the Russians had made it impossible for the Germans to concentrate all their efforts on the Western Front. In addition, they had provided the French and British with sufficient breathing space to call up reservists, begin to train new recruits and bring to Europe the armies being raised in the British Empire – Australians, New Zealanders, Canadians, Indians and South Africans. Now Russia herself was in desperate need of help from her allies.

What went wrong on the Eastern Front?

In spite of their superiority in numbers, during the early stages of the war the Russian army gained only limited success against the Austro-Hungarians in Galicia before being badly mauled by the Germans in East Prussia and forced to retreat. Its disasters were accompanied by calamitous losses. What went wrong?

In the first place, the soldiers of the so-called Russian 'steamroller' army lacked adequate training and were poorly led and whilst Grand Duke Nicholas was considered to have done as well as circumstances allowed, his subordinates were ineffective to the point of being pathetic. Recruits drafted in as replacements for the losses were often sent to the front line without weapons and had to use agricultural implements such as scythes and pitchforks or wait to take weapons from the dead and wounded. In addition, they were inadequately equipped, clothed and fed and their armies possessed inadequate artillery and very few aircraft. During their offensives they still depended heavily on the success of the old-fashioned cavalry charges but even such skilled horsemen as the Cossacks were no match for German machine gunners. Of the slaughter, Hindenburg wrote, 'Sometimes we had to remove the mounds of enemy corpses from before our trenches in order to get a clear field of fire against fresh assaulting waves.' The historian John Erickson summed it up adequately when he wrote, 'The Russian infantryman, ill-equipped and under-fed, performed great feats of endurance and showed raw, unflinching courage, but manpower could not continually match the murderous enemy firepower.'

Vladimir Sukhomilov, the Russian Minister of War and a man said to 'have grown fat on inefficiency', must carry the blame for the appalling state of affairs. A friend of Tsar Nicholas and one of the favourites at court, he was described as being 'short and soft with a cat-like face, neat whiskers and beard and with an ingratiating almost feline manner that captivated those he set out to please'. He retained favour by being servile, flattering and entertaining and instead of discussing important military matters he preferred to tell jokes and be a figure of fun. He was partly responsible for his country's ill-advised entry into the war in 1914 and assured the Russian government, the Duma, that their army was ready for war and would be able to deal with any demands placed on it. From the start, Sukhomilov was at loggerheads with Grand Duke Nicholas and as the war progressed the two men came to hate each other. The Grand Duke blamed the disasters of 1914 and 1915 on Sukhomilov's apathy and incompetence and some Russians went as far as to suggest that Sukhomilov was secretly in the employment of the Germans. This was certainly not the case but unknowingly he did have two German spies on his staff and had borrowed sums of money from them. In the summer of 1915, a commission of inquiry found him guilty of incompetence and he was dismissed. Shortly afterwards he was tried, convicted for corruption and treason and sent to prison. On his release, he moved abroad and died in Berlin in 1926.

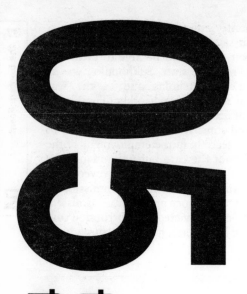

05

the Dardanelles fiasco

This chapter will cover:
- the differing views on the need for a campaign in the eastern Mediterranean
- the failure of the naval attack on the Dardanelles
- the preparations for the Gallipoli campaign and the involvement of the ANZACs
- the nature of the Gallipoli campaign
- some unusual episodes during the campaign
- the reasons for the failure of the Gallipoli campaign.

'Fair broke the day this morning,
Against the Dardanelles;
The breeze blew soft, the morn's cheeks
Were cold as cold as shells
But other shells were waiting
Across the Aegean Sea,
Shrapnel and high explosive,
Shells and hells for me.'

(From an untitled poem by Patrick Shaw-Stewart,
1888–1917)

Easterners versus Westerners

The entry of Turkey into the war meant that Britain had to take steps to protect her interests in the Persian Gulf and Egypt where the Suez Canal, her all important lifeline to India and the Far East, had to be safeguarded at all costs. The involvement of

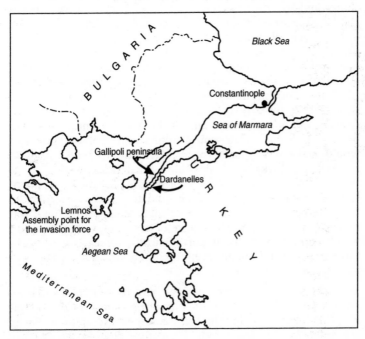

figure 10 the strategic importance of the Dardanelles and the Gallipoli peninsula

Turkey was also significant to developments on other fronts. During the early months of 1915, two major problems confronted the Allies – what steps should be taken to break the deadlock on the Western Front and how could Britain and France best help to sustain Russia's flagging war effort and ensure that she remained in the war? A diversionary attack might provide a solution, but then there would be the question of where. Allied generals and politicians were divided on the whole issue.

In Britain, the War Council discussed different strategies. A plan to land along the Belgian coast behind the German lines was considered but quickly discounted before David Lloyd George, the Chancellor of the Exchequer and soon to be Minister of Munitions, and Winston Churchill, the First Lord of the Admiralty, argued that it was time for Britain to use her naval might to turn the tide without the further loss of millions of lives. An urgent appeal for help from Grand Duke Nicholas in Russia made an expedition against the Turks the most obvious choice and so Lloyd George and Churchill backed by Maurice Hankey, the Secretary of the War Council, and Admiral Sir John Fisher, made plans for 'a great amphibious operation' in the eastern Mediterranean. Collectively referred to as Easterners, they argued for a campaign aimed at securing the Dardanelles, the narrow straits that separated that part of Turkey in Europe from the Turkish mainland. The Dardanelles was also the seaway that by way of the Sea of Marmara connected the Aegean Sea, at the eastern end of the Mediterranean, with the Black Sea. Such a plan would fulfil two important aims – it would make it necessary for the Germans to send troops to reinforce the Turks and so possibly weaken their position on the Western Front and it would also bring into play the Royal Navy. Britain's greatest asset could be used to force a sea route to beleaguered Russia and make it possible to supply her with war materials and also give the chance of capturing Constantinople, which Churchill boldly, if unrealistically, forecast would take three weeks, and might even force Turkey out of the war altogether.

The scheme was controversial and had its opponents. These, known as Westerners, were mainly British and French generals in the High Command who were firmly of the opinion that in the long run, the war would be won or lost on the Western Front. They thought that there should be no slackening in the Allied efforts against Germany and claimed that the Dardanelles venture would at best, be a sideshow. Lord Kitchener, the British Minister for War, went further and insisted that no men be taken from the Western Front since this might weaken the Allied position there. Eventually a compromise was agreed by which an attempt would be made to force the Dardanelles by using naval power only. The British War Council resolved that the Royal Navy should 'prepare an expedition to bombard the Gallipoli peninsula with Constantinople as its objective'. Agreed without adequate consultation with military leaders or a realistic consideration of the difficulties posed by studying maps of the region, it was an ill-advised scheme. Furthermore no investigation had been held to discover if sufficient ships were available for the operation. The historian A. J. P. Taylor summed up the situation when he wrote, 'The War Council assumed that great armadas could waft non-existent armies to the ends of the earth in the twinkling of an eye' (*Struggle for the Mastery of Europe*, 1954).

The naval attack on the Dardanelles

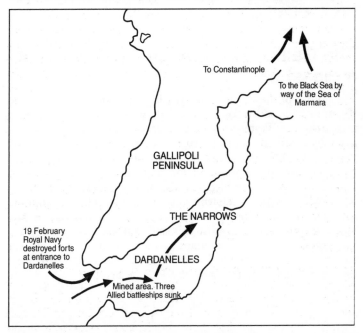

figure 11 March 1915 – the naval attack on the Dardanelles

The first attack came when naval units under Admiral Sackville Carden attacked and largely destroyed the Turkish forts guarding the entrance to the Dardanelles but bad weather prevented their work being completed. Next mine sweeping trawlers manned by civilian crews and commanded by naval officers were sent to clear Turkish mines laid at the approach to the stretch of waterway known as the Narrows. Here, at a point where the channel was barely two kilometres (1.2 miles) wide, the Turkish guns situated on both sides of the water opened fire on the trawlers and forced them to retreat before the mines had all been cleared. A further problem arose when the sickly Admiral Carden fell ill and had to be replaced by his second-in-command, Admiral John de Robeck. A month later, an Allied fleet made up of 18 ships, many of them obsolete and considered expendable, sailed towards the Narrows with the intention of bombarding the Turkish gun positions and disrupting their communications. At first things seemed to go well until one French and two British battleships struck mines. Altogether the Allies lost six battleships and the disheartened de Robeck refused to continue the attack without adequate military support.

The Gallipoli campaign – the onset of a disaster

The failure of the naval attack finally persuaded Kitchener that the use of ground troops was essential. To avoid withdrawing men from the Western Front, a force of some 70,000 men was assembled consisting of the Australian and New Zealand Army Corps – the ANZACs – as well as British and French units. The force, under the command of a British general, Sir Ian Hamilton, was assembled on the Greek island of Lemnos. Although a man of charm and with a wealth of military experience, Hamilton was to prove an unimaginative and indecisive military leader and it is said that his knowledge of the Dardanelles was limited to maps in a tourist guidebook. He was to prove a far from ideal choice. From the start there were problems caused by the lack of adequate artillery and medical supplies and the fact that to make good the shortfall in landing craft, vessels had to be bought from the Greeks. Furthermore, with so much activity going on, the Turks were well aware that something was being planned.

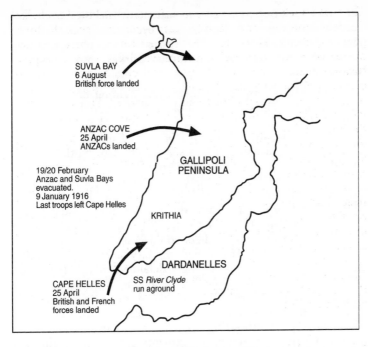

figure 12 the Gallipoli campaign – April 1915–January 1916

The intention was to invade and occupy the Gallipoli peninsula and to achieve this, British and French forces would land on the tip of the peninsula at Cape Helles and the ANZACs further to the north near Gaba Tepe. In an attempt to mislead the Turks, a series of diversionary operations were planned but as the Allied intention became patently clear, the Turkish army, commanded by the German general, Liman von Sanders, dug in, improved their defences and transferred additional forces to the peninsula. The omens for the Allies were not good.

At dawn on 25 April 1915, the first troops ashore were the Australians. Either human error or the strength of the tide led them to land two kilometres (1.2 miles) north of the intended beach and they found themselves in a cove, later known as Anzac Cove, surrounded by high cliffs. Their landing was only lightly opposed and they were able to press ahead inland until strong Turkish resistance forced them back. At the time, the Turkish commander was Mustapha Kemal, a skilled military tactician and a born leader of men, and his inspired leadership was to play an important part in sustaining Turkish morale and the events that were to lead to their eventual victory. Later, as Kemal Ataturk, he became the leader of his country and was responsible for reforms that turned Turkey into a modern secular state.

The Australians now found themselves fighting desperately to hold on to the cliffs that overlooked their original landing site and the following day, the beach became a shambles as men wandered aimlessly about and stores piled up on the sand. It was, said one journalist, 'like a shipwreck'. During the months ahead, this area was to witness some of the most ferocious fighting of the Gallipoli campaign. On most other beaches, the landings were more successful but at Cape Helles, the Allies suffered another disaster. Here, the plan was for an old collier, a coal-carrying ship the *River Clyde*, to be run aground close to an old fort so that the soldiers could easily wade ashore and storm the beaches. The Allied military commanders didn't realize that the area was strongly defended by the Turks and that the water was too deep for the men to wade ashore. As a result, hundreds were either drowned or mown down by machine-gun fire as they tried to scramble from their grounded ship. On a neighbouring beach, men came under such murderous fire that later reinforcements 'waded ashore through a sea that was literally crimson with blood'. From a ship offshore, General Hunter-Weston, known to his men as 'Hunter-Bunter', seemed unaware of the catastrophe and continued to order his troops to land on an already hopelessly overcrowded beach whilst Hamilton, at his headquarters on board the battleship HMS *Queen Elizabeth* described the scene as 'too monstrous, too cold blooded; like watching gladiators from the dress circle'. Even so and in spite of many disturbing reports, he decided not to interfere with the decisions being made by 'the men on the spot'.

The remainder of the campaign

During the months that followed, the British and French on Cape Helles launched a series of offensives in an attempt to advance further inland but they suffered considerable losses and made only limited gains. At Anzac Cove, the front line changed little as the Australians and New Zealanders struggled to hang on to their narrow bridgehead. Unable to break out and with the Turks unable to drive them back into the sea, a stalemate was reached. With the opposed trenches often less than 100 metres (328 feet) apart, the fighting was usually hand-to-hand, grim and bloody and one Turkish attack against the ANZAC positions was so murderous that a truce had to be called to allow both sides to bring in their wounded and bury their dead. Trenches were sometimes blocked with the bodies of the dead and dying whilst the smell of decaying corpses was ever present and overpowering. The soldiers in the trenches were infested with lice and fleas and pestered by hordes of rats and when eating had to blow away swarms of flies before they could put food in their mouths. It was claimed that flies caused more casualties than bullets as men suffered from malaria, dysentery, a form of chronic diarrhoea, and other stomach disorders. Open wounds were soon covered with maggots and those transferred to the hospital ships sometimes found themselves being treated by veterinary surgeons and unqualified orderlies. A shortage of fit men meant that the wounded were often returned to the front line before they were fully recovered. During the summer months, the blazing sun made the heat overbearing and water was always in short supply. In one instance, a New Zealander sentenced to death for desertion was sent back to the front line where he fought bravely yet the following morning he was still executed as planned. With 'Johnny Turk' proving himself a far better soldier than expected, the Allied front line positions were constantly being shelled and any reckless movement was likely to attract the attention of a Turkish sniper. A final attempt was made to end the deadlock when Allied soldiers landed to the north at Suvla Bay, a move that was intended to coincide with an attempted breakout by those at Anzac Cove. For once the Turks were taken by surprise and the men on the two Allied beaches were able to link up.

Some unusual episodes

Born in 1892 at Durham in the north of England, John Simpson Kirkpatrick was 17 when he left home to work as a stoker on-board ship. He eventually settled in Queensland, Australia where he gained a reputation for brawling and a love of animals. At the start of the war, he enlisted in the Australian army under the name John Simpson and served in the 3rd Field Ambulance. Sent to Gallipoli, he landed at Anzac Cove and soon found himself a donkey. He used the animal to carry wounded men down from the front line to the beach and on his return journeys he took much-needed water supplies to the forward positions. Acting on his own initiative, he and his donkey became a familiar sight at Anzac Cove and, known for his whistling and wisecracking, he was ever cheerful and seemed oblivious to the dangers of snipers and shellfire. Simpson's bravery and good humour made him a legend until he was killed by machine-gun fire as he helped two wounded men down to the beach. Buried at Anzac Cove, he was later recommended for a Victoria Cross but the award was never made. He is still remembered with great affection by Australians and recently he featured on one of their postage stamps.

It was King George V's idea that some of the men serving on his Sandringham estate should form a company to serve in the war. The Sandringham Company, as it was known, was largely made up of servants, grooms and gardeners and became part of the 1/5th Battalion of the Norfolk Regiment and was commanded by Captain Frank Beck, the King's land agent on the estate. In August 1915 the Company landed at Suvla Bay. On 12 August 1915, Beck led his men forward across a section of the Suvla Plain towards the Turkish lines and they were never seen again. Afterwards rumours abounded about the 'vanished battalion', and some eyewitnesses went as far as to claim that they saw a yellow mist descend that formed a cloud and carried the men heavenward to safety. As was later discovered, the truth was far more ugly. The fact was that the men ran into a hail of machine-gun fire and the survivors, when surrounded, surrendered. As prisoners of war they were taken to a nearby barn and there in turn shot in the head. In 1999, the BBC made a film *All the King's Men* which told of this event with David Jason playing the part of Captain Frank Beck.

The end of the campaign and the evacuation

In London and Paris there was increasing concern about the conduct of the Gallipoli campaign since it had failed to achieve its aims and the Allies were suffering heavy losses. Winston Churchill was blamed for conceiving the idea in the first place and was forced to resign. In Britain, people began to question the ability of Hamilton and he was recalled and replaced by General Sir Charles Monro. The new commander immediately came to the conclusion that the campaign had to end, and the Gallipoli peninsula evacuated. A bitter Churchill commented, 'He came, he saw, he capitulated'. Although the forced withdrawal from the Dardanelles was a blow to Allied prestige, the final stage of the campaign proved a complete success. Ingenious plans were made to confuse the Turks so that they thought the Allied front line was still being strongly defended and then during the course of just two nights, the troops slipped quietly away from their positions at Anzac and Sulva. For a few weeks the British and French troops remained at Cape Helles until they too were finally evacuated and the disastrous episode came to an end.

The Dardanelles campaign – some considerations

General Hamilton once said 'The most fatal heresy of war is to believe that battles can be won without heavy losses'. The Dardanelles campaign was a dismal failure – it achieved nothing but still incurred heavy losses – and there is no doubt that the leadership of the Allied forces was inferior to that of the Turks. The intellectual Hamilton turned out to be more a frustrated poet than a military commander and he, together with other Allied commanders, completely underestimated the fighting qualities of Turkish soldiers. Many of them may have been illiterate peasants but they fought with great bravery to rid their country of the unwelcome invaders.

As the campaign progressed, the Australians and New Zealanders came to regard it as a 'British bungle'. The ANZACs disliked Hamilton intensely and thought he represented the worst of the British class system; they also considered General Hunter-Weston, alias Hunter-Bunter, 'a worthless buffoon'. His case was not helped by such worthless comments as 'Casualties? What do I care about casualties?' The ANZACs own commanding officer, Major-General William Birdwood, was certainly a far more gifted officer who showed a greater concern for the welfare of his men. The Australians and New Zealanders did not like the 'spit and polish' mentality of the British army and were slow to salute officers, particularly British officers. Only four men were shot at dawn by firing squads during the campaign largely because the Australians refused to allow their soldiers to be subject to the death penalty.

The Dardanelles campaign ruined political and military reputations and wasted thousands of lives. The total number of Allied casualties came to just over 250,000 and of these, 21,555 were British, 10,000 French, 8,702 Australians and 2,701 New Zealanders. No one knows for certain how many Turks lost their lives but the number is thought to be similar to that of the Allies. For Australia and New Zealand, the Dardanelles campaign was the most significant event in their history. Today, those 'pages of history written in the blood of their soldiers' are regarded as the birth of their national awareness and even their nationhood.

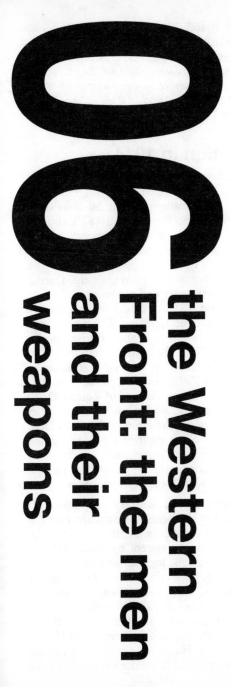

06

the Western Front: the men and their weapons

This chapter will cover:
- the recruitment of men for the British army
- army life
- British, French and German soldiers
- the weapons used in the trenches
- other weapons introduced during the war.

'This bloody steel
Has killed a man.
I heard him squeal
As on I ran.'

(From *The Bayonet*
by Wilfred Gibson, 1887–1930)

The general situation in 1914

There can be no doubt that at the start of the war Germany possessed the best trained and equipped army on mainland Europe. The French army, still suffering from an inferiority complex after its humiliation by the Prussians in 1870, though adequate in numbers, could not match the efficiency of the Germans. Russia could call on massive manpower reserves but did not have generals of any quality to lead them nor the necessary means to equip and support them in the field. During the nineteenth century, the British army had not enjoyed the best of fortunes. Between 1854 and 1856, it had fought a largely inconclusive war against Russia, the Crimean War, and a year later struggled to put down a rebellion against British rule in India, the Indian mutiny. In 1879, at the Battle of Isandlwana in South Africa, the British army suffered its greatest ever defeat at the hands of native warriors, the Zulu, but later on the same day, this was in part redeemed by the heroic defence of Rorke's Drift. General Gordon's expedition to the Sudan in 1885 ended in disaster until Kitchener reconquered the country 13 years later. The British army also failed to cover itself in glory during the Boer Wars and it was only after Boer women and children had been rounded up and placed in concentration camps that the last Boer resistance ended and they were forced to seek peace.

Against the expressed wishes of the military establishment, significant changes took place in the British army when Edward Cardwell, the Secretary for War during the 1870s, abolished the 'purchase system', a long-established system by which officers bought their rank. Infantry regiments, long known by numbers, changed to county titles so that, for example, 14th Foot became the West Yorkshire Regiment, and 28th Foot became the Gloucestershire Regiment. Cardwell also abolished flogging as a punishment in the army and reduced the number of years that a soldier could be expected to serve abroad. Between 1905 and 1912, the Secretary for War, R. B. Haldane, introduced a further series of organizational reforms that placed the command of the army under a General Staff and created a Territorial Army. He also provided for the rapid mobilization of an expeditionary force that could be sent abroad with little notice and it was this, the British Expeditionary Force (BEF), that first crossed to France in 1914. Unfortunately many of Haldane's reforms were largely copied from the German system and, accused of having German sympathies, he was forced to resign.

The British situation in 1914

In common with all the other belligerent European powers, at the outbreak of war Britain experienced a surge of patriotic fervour accompanied by a rush of volunteers keen to serve their 'King and Country'. The government's first action was to send a well-trained army of regular soldiers to France, the BEF, and these were soon to be joined by Reservists, those who had once been in the army and were liable to recall, and Territorials. The 64-year-old Field Marshal, Lord Kitchener, was made Secretary for War but in the long run it would prove an unhappy appointment.

Kitchener realized that the conflict would not 'be over by Christmas' and launched a recruiting campaign aimed at raising a new army of 500,000 volunteers capable of fighting a lengthy war. Great pressure was put on men to get them into khaki. Kitchener's famous poster, 'Your Country Needs You' immediately appealed to one's sense of patriotism and was used to great effect. Others used subtle emotional blackmail – a girl asking her father, 'Daddy, what did you do in the war?' was typical. Girls handed white feathers, a sign of cowardice, to men of military age who were still out of uniform and the opening line of a popular music-hall song of the day ran, 'We don't want to lose you but we think you ought to go'. In churches and chapels, clergy used their sermons to urge men to volunteer for military service. Across the country men wishing to join the Colours besieged recruiting offices with under-age youths and over-age men using all sorts of ploys to deceive the recruiting officers. It was quite usual for men to join with their friends, work mates and others from the same trade and they formed the so-called 'Pals Battalions' such as the 'Accrington Pals', the 'Cardiff Pals', and the 'Grimsby Chums'. Clerks and office workers came together to form units such as the 'Newcastle Commercials' whilst the 'Glasgow Tramways' was made up of transport workers from the city. One battalion consisted of members of the Boys' Brigade whilst another was made up entirely of public schoolboys. Kitchener was not entirely happy with the idea of 'Pals Battalions' since he feared that men's loyalties might be more to their locality than their regiment and country. By the end of 1914, some 1.19 million men had come forward and so great was the number of volunteers that it was not necessary to introduce conscription until January 1916. Unfortunately, the rush to join up caused problems with recruits having to be accommodated in makeshift camps, and with insufficient uniforms to go around, men had to drill in their civilian clothes with imitation rifles. There was also an acute shortage of officers and this meant that officers serving in the Indian Army and young men fresh from Officer Training Corps at public schools and universities had to be drafted in to make up for the shortfall.

'Joining up' – army life and organization

When a volunteer first joined up, he was allocated an army number, 'kitted out', provided with his uniform, clothing and equipment and given his 'dog-tags' – identity discs bearing his name, army number and religion that were worn around the neck. He would then complete his basic training at an army camp where he would be taught how to drill, sent on route marches and instructed in the use of weapons. At the start of the war, he could join a regiment of his choice, usually his own county regiment, but as the war progressed and casualties mounted he would be more likely to be drafted to a unit in need of replacements. Apart from the county regiments, there were also regiments of guards, such as the Coldstream and Grenadier Guards, and cavalry regiments with distinctive names such as the Dragoons, Hussars and Lancers. The infantry was supported by a wide range of specialist units and corps such as the 'gunners' of the Royal Artillery, the 'sappers' of The Royal Engineers and the Royal Army Medical Corps. Later in the war, the Tank Regiment and the Royal Flying Corps were to appear.

The organization and chain of command in the army were complicated. On joining, a new recruit would be allocated to one of the battalions of his regiment. A battalion consisted of something approaching 1,000 men and was commanded by a lieutenant-colonel or colonel. During the First World War so many men rushed to join the army that it became necessary to create many extra battalions. Hence a soldier might say that he was serving in the 7th Royal West Kents or the 16th Lancashire Fusiliers. Within his battalion, a soldier would be allocated to a company, within his company to a platoon and within his platoon to a section.

A new recruit would have to get used to the daily routine of the army – parades, cleaning his boots and polishing his buttons, kit inspections and the round of unpleasant duties given as punishment for minor offences. He had to learn to recognize and salute officers and be aware of the various bugle-calls – reveille at daybreak, the call to the cookhouse at mealtimes and the 'Last Post' for lights out. Many young soldiers became homesick and found army discipline excessively demanding. A colonel is said to have commented, 'They're a rough crowd and a tough crowd: but they're a stout crowd. By gad! We'll make them a credit to the old regiment yet.'

Within the army, a battalion would represent a relatively small unit. Battalions were drawn together from different regiments with artillery and other support units to form a brigade. Brigades were combined to form a division and divisions were organized into corps. Finally corps were brought together to form an army. Armies operating together in the same battle area would be placed under the command of a field marshal and during the course of the war, the British armies in France were first commanded by Field Marshal Sir John French and later by Field Marshal Sir Douglas Haig. The commander-in-chief and his staff would be based at general headquarters (GHQ) that would be situated well behind the front line and from here, they would dictate the course of the war and the fate of thousands of soldiers. Generally speaking, the most senior officers found in the front line would be the battalion commanders, the lieutenant-colonels and colonels but staff officers or 'top brass' as they were called, seldom visited the front line.

The British soldier

The vast majority of the men who joined the army served as private soldiers or privates. Immediately above them were non-commissioned officers or NCOs of which the most junior was a lance corporal and then came corporals and sergeants. Their rank was indicated by chevrons (V-shaped stripes) on the arm. Immediately above the NCOs were the warrant officers, the company and regimental sergeant majors who were usually noted for their dedication to discipline, their insistence on 'spit and polish' and their ability to shout on the parade ground! Officers, as the term is usually understood, were commissioned officers and such men were said to hold the king's commission that had to be acknowledged by other soldiers with a salute. The most junior officers were subalterns, that is second lieutenants and lieutenants. If promotion came, they might eventually be promoted to captain, major, colonel and, at the very top, to that of general and field marshal. During the First World War, stars (pips) and crowns on the cuff of his uniform indicated a commissioned officer's rank. Almost all officers were drawn from the upper-classes and were public-school educated and promotion from the ranks was unusual. However, as the war progressed and the number of casualties increased, it became more common. Many young subalterns serving in the trenches were aged 18 and only just out of school.

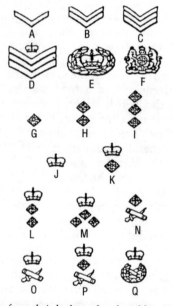

Non-commissioned officers and warrent officers wore their badges of rank on their sleeves. Officers carried their badges of rank on their tunic cuffs.

A lance-corporal
B corporal
C sergeant
D colour sergeant
E company sergeant major
F regimental sergeant major
G second lieutenant
H lieutenant
I captain
J major
K lieutenant-colonel
L colonel
M brigadier-general
N major-general
O lieutenant-general
P general
Q field marshal

Apart from their badges of rank, soldiers wore regimental badges in their caps and regimental shoulder titles. They also carried patches and signs to indicate their brigade and division.

Badges of rank in the British army

Ordinary British soldiers wore khaki-coloured battledress made out of rough, serge material and the tunic was single breasted and fastened at the neck. The trousers extended down to puttees, strips of cloth wound spirally around the leg from the ankle to just below the knee, and for headgear, they had cloth peaked caps. Stoutly made army boots caused men to suffer agonizing blisters particularly after marching for miles along the *pavé*, French cobbled roads. Each soldier was also provided with webbing equipment, a belt, braces and buckles to which he could attach a haversack, pack, ammunition pouches, a waterbottle carrier, a 'frog' to hold his bayonet and a carrier for his entrenching tool. Steel helmets were first issued in February 1916 but were not in general use until a year later. Officers' uniforms were made of superior, worsted-type material, barathea, and included a jacket with patch pockets that opened at the neck to show a shirt and tie, above breeches and riding boots or leggings. The most distinctive item of clothing of an officer's uniform was his 'Sam Browne' – a leather shoulder strap, belt and revolver holster named after General Sir Samuel Browne who first designed it. Both officers and men carried canes known as 'swagger sticks'.

In order to be accepted as a volunteer, a man had to be physically fit, over 1.6 metres (5.2 feet) tall and aged 18 to 38 or up to 45 if he had previous military service. Later, men below the minimum height requirement were recruited and nicknamed 'Bantams', and they formed special units for undersized men and were often subject to ridicule. Eventually the name was discontinued and the units disbanded. A volunteer, who was expected to enlist for the duration of the war, received 35 pence a week with food and clothing provided free. To support his wife and children, he had to contribute an allotment to a Separation Allowance so that his wife received 62 pence weekly – 45 pence allowance plus her husband's own 17 pence allotment. The total payable to a wife with two children was 87 pence weekly. Once enrolled, a soldier became subject to military law, King's Regulations. It should be remembered that a man's reasons for joining the army were not always motivated by patriotism or the desire to serve one's 'King and Country'. There were also other considerations such as the need to escape the drudgery of their everyday work, slum living conditions and to escape the threat of unemployment. In 1914, the average wage of a manual worker was about one pound a week and half of that would be spent on rent! The average weekly expenditure of a working man's family was about 50 pence so that there was seldom anything left over for any extras or even the smallest extravagance. Unemployment brought with it dire poverty and even those in work all too often lived in poverty in overcrowded, insanitary slums where a high death rate was an accepted fact of life. For such men, the demands and risks of army life were not such a bad deal. There were also those who were taken in by the belief that it would be a short war – 'over by Christmas' – and had volunteered in order not to miss out on what they judged to be an adventure with the promise of foreign travel and the chance to meet French *mesdemoiselles*.

British, French and German soldiers – a comparison

A British soldier fully dressed in Field Marching Order would be heavily burdened with packs and equipment that would vary according to season and whether or not he was on the march. Normally he would be expected to carry a third of his own weight, about 35 kilos (77 pounds). As the war progressed his burden was increased by the addition of a steel helmet and gas mask.

At the start of the war, a French soldier was dressed in a dark blue *capote*, a long cloak-like tunic, with red trousers and a red and blue forage cap or *kepi*. Such colourful clothing clearly had disadvantages and before the end of 1914 a far more modest blue-grey uniform had replaced it.

The most famous item of clothing of a German soldier would have been his *pickelhaube* or spiked helmet. His uniform, field grey tunic and trousers, was worn with calf-length jackboots. During 1916, his style of helmet changed to a *Stahlhelm* that gave added protection to the back of the neck.

Weapons used in the trenches

The main weapon of the British soldier was a .303, bolt action Lee-Enfield rifle with a magazine that held ten rounds of ammunition. An experienced infantryman could fire 25 rounds a minute whilst skilled sharpshooters and snipers had rifles with specially fitted telescopic sights. The most popular German rifle was the *Mauser* whilst the French used the *Lebel*. British officers carried Webley revolvers and the Germans, the famous *Lugars*.

Every soldier also carried a bayonet that was simply a blade attached to the end of the rifle and used against the enemy in close hand-to-hand fighting. The British bayonet was knife shaped, the French, pencil shaped whilst the Germans used a 'saw-back' blade with a row of teeth on the back edge.

Far more devastating than the rifle was the machine gun. The machine guns used by both sides during the war were largely based on the original design of the American inventor Hiram Maxim. At the start of the war the main British machine gun was the Lewis gun, the so-called 'Queen of the battlefield' which was mounted on a bipod and fed by a pan-shaped magazine fitted on the top. More lethal was the Vickers machine gun which was water cooled with a metal jacket around the barrel and could fire 600 rounds a minute. Mounted on a tripod, it could be set to fire along a fixed line between two points and this meant that there was no need to aim and machine gunners just swept the area ahead with a hail of bullets. Little wonder the machine gun was nicknamed the 'Devil's Sprinkler'. The machine gun used by the French was the Hotchkiss and by the Germans, the *Maschinengewehr*.

Another weapon much used in trench warfare was the hand grenade that was thrown at the enemy. The British Mills grenade, which was made of cast iron and segmented so that it broke into pieces of shrapnel more easily when it detonated, was fitted with a timed fuse that was connected to a lever held in place by a pin. The pin had to be removed in order for it to explode. Later the grenade was modified so that it could be fired from a rifle. Germans used the *Stielhandgranate* or 'stick bomb' that had a handle and the *Kugelhandgranate* which was ball shaped and known to the British as the 'pineapple grenade'. There were also trench mortars that were fixed to a base, shaped like a drainpipe and used to throw shells short distances into the enemy positions.

Flame throwers were first used by the Germans. At first their *Flammenwerfers* were primitive, used ordinary petrol and were very unreliable. Canisters were liable to explode and so cause the user to perish in the flames of his own weapon. So hated were flame throwers with their terrifying bursts of liquid fire that prisoners of war thought to have been involved in their use were liable to be shot out of hand.

Finally, when all other forms of weaponry had been used up, men fought hand-to-hand. As they wrestled they used their fists, clubs, entrenching tools and anything else that was available.

Other weapons

Artillery played a major role throughout the war with both sides using a great variety of field guns and howitzers that fired shrapnel, high explosive and gas shells. Field guns were intended to fire shells across open country whilst howitzers, with their higher trajectory, could drop shells into hollows and trenches. Some shells disintegrated into small fragments called shrapnel that caused horrendous injuries whilst high explosive shells caused enormous material damage and left massive craters. Guns were classified according to their calibre, that is the diameter or bore of the barrel, and shells according to their weight. British artillery included the 18-pounder field gun with a range of six kilometres (3.7 miles), the 60-pounder field gun with a range of nearly ten kilometres (six miles) and the massive 30 cm (12-inch) howitzer that had to be moved by rail and had a range of 13 kilometres (eight miles). None of these could match the German long-barrelled gun that had a staggering range of 65 kilometres (40 miles). Nicknamed 'Big Bertha', supposedly after the manufacturer's wife, this most famous Krupp-built howitzer could send a shell weighing a tonne over 13 kilometres (eight miles). Exploding shells not only killed and maimed but also buried men alive and caused a nervous disorder known as 'shell shock'. Empty shell cases became one of the most common souvenirs of the war and even today can still be found in many homes.

Although outlawed by the Geneva Convention of 1899, the Germans first used gas as a weapon of war on the Ypres salient in 1915. The first to be used was chlorine gas that came in clouds visible to the eye and had a distinctive smell described as a mixture of pineapple and pepper. It produced unpleasant side effects and caused soldiers to suffer a lingering death by suffocation. Later in the war phosgene gas was introduced which was also derived from chlorine but being 18 times stronger was far worse. It had the smell of rotting fish and since it was heavier than air, it was liable to linger in shell craters and trenches for days after first being dispersed. However it was dicloroethyl sulphide or mustard gas that became the most feared. Its effects were not immediately apparent but after some hours blisters appeared that affected the eyes and bronchial tubes so that affected soldiers were liable to be blinded or drown in their own blood. In 1915, a reporter for *The New York Tribune* described the effects of 'violent nausea and faintness followed by utter collapse. It is believed that the Germans, who charged in behind the gas, met no resistance at all, the French at their front being virtually paralysed'. In the trenches, empty shell cases were used as gongs to warn of the approach of gas. To start with, soldiers had no protection other than the ammonia in their own urine and bicarbonate of soda, if it was available, to part neutralize the effects of the gas. Soon many thousands of specially manufactured protective pads of cotton waste wrapped in muslin and held in place by tape were sent to the front as a stop gap before the first gas masks or respirators arrived. The first were grotesque bags with goggle-type eye pieces that covered the whole head and these were followed by more refined respirators which consisted of a mask that fitted tightly around the face connected by a tube to a canister hung in front of the wearer's body. The canister contained charcoal through which the poison gas filtered. The gas masks were cumbersome, difficult to wear and gave only limited protection. None were totally effective against mustard gas.

Tanks and the need for mobility

A few imaginative officers in the British army recognized the need to develop a mechanized armoured vehicle capable of passing through barbed wire to provide cover for troops advancing across no man's land towards the enemy's positions. Lieutenant-Colonel Ernest Swinton suggested using armoured tractors to carry infantry and guns and although the idea was rejected, a Landships Committee was set up to investigate the possibility of designing armoured vehicles. Following lengthy delays, the prototype of the first landship appeared. Nicknamed 'Little Willie', it was no more than a large metal box on tracks but in order to maintain secrecy, the model was officially called Tank Mark I. As a result, the name 'tank' later came to be applied to similar types of vehicle the world over. Although 'Little Willie' had many shortcomings since it could not cross a gap more than two and a half metres (8.2 feet) wide and had a maximum speed of only five kilometres (three miles) an hour, it was to be the basic model on which future tanks would be designed. The first variation was called 'Mother', it weighed 28 tonnes, had a crew of eight but its maximum speed remained the same and the British High Command remained far from impressed. Kitchener dismissed it as a 'pretty mechanical toy' and others expressed the view that the war could not possibly be won by such machines. When the first tanks went into production, Mark I came in two varieties – male tanks armed with two six-pounder guns at each side and female tanks with four Vickers machine guns mounted on the sides. Later a wooden beam was attached to the front to help it cross fields of mud and a wire canopy stretched across the top in order to deflect grenades thrown at it. For the crews of the tanks conditions inside were horrendous with the engine giving off stifling fumes and heat, the deafening noise and the crew being thrown around as the tank lurched from side to side. If the tank commander wanted to communicate with those outside, he had to open the door and shout through a megaphone. The first British tanks arrived in France in August 1916.

During the course of the war, whatever advances were made in the technology of warfare by one side were soon copied by the other. Although the Germans were first to use poison gas and flame throwers, both were in use by the British and French armies by the end of 1915. It is interesting to note that in October 1918, a 29-year-old corporal serving in a Bavarian infantry regiment was temporarily blinded by British gas – his name was Adolf Hitler. Likewise, the Germans worked to design their own tank and this resulted in the development of the A7V *Sturmpanzerwagen* that weighed 33 tonnes, required a crew of 18 and had a top speed of 12 kilometres (7.5 miles) an hour. Only 20 were built and the majority of tanks used by the Germans during the war were those captured from the British.

The role of horses

No account of the First World War would be complete without mention of the important part played by horses on the Western, Eastern and Italian Fronts and in the campaigns against the Turks. Tens of thousands of horses were employed in a range of different roles and thousands were killed or so badly mutilated that they had to be put down. The cavalry was considered by many to be the elite of the army and many senior officers including French, Haig, Allenby, Hamilton and Robertson were drawn from its ranks. At the start of the war, units of cavalry – Dragoons, Hussars and Lancers – crossed to France and those in command were convinced that the cavalry still had a major part to play in offensive warfare. British cavalrymen together with French *Curassiers* were soon involved in skirmishes with their German counterparts, the *Uhlans*. It was hoped that the cavalry units would be the shock-troops of the battlefield and it was intended that they would charge, breach the enemy's positions and then deploy in the countryside beyond. The

Cavalry Training Manual of 1907 still championed the horse as the main offence weapon of war and stated, 'It must be accepted as a principle that the rifle, effective as it is, cannot replace the effect produced by the speed of a horse, the magnetism of the charge and the terror of cold steel.' Although the cavalry played some part in the retreat from Mons and the Battle of the Marne, it was gradually realized that the day of the charge was over and instead their use was limited to that of scouting and reconnaissance. In 1915, an impatient Field Marshal French wrote, 'How I would love to have a real go at them with lots of cavalry … and run them down to earth'. As the war progressed, the limitations of cavalry against machine-guns and other advances in the technology of warfare became increasingly obvious and although held in reserve on the Somme in 1916, cavalry units never had an opportunity to exploit a breakthrough. Elsewhere in Mesopotamia and Palestine, cavalry was used with some success but on the Western Front it ceased to be an effective fighting force and by the end of the war most cavalrymen had abandoned their horses to become infantrymen.

The most important role played by horses was in providing mobility. Most artillery was horse drawn and horses were used to move wagon of munitions, supplies and provisions from the rear to the forward areas. In performing these duties, they had to survive on insufficient fodder and were often overworked so that once exhausted to the point where they could go no further, they were shot out of hand. Close to the front line, soldiers became distressed at the sight of horses still moving with their entrails exposed and one senior officer witnessing the slaughter of horses and mules commented, 'Human corpses are all very well but it seems wrong for animals to be dragged into the war like this'. The demand for horses became so great that at home they had to be requisitioned in spite of the protestations of their owners.

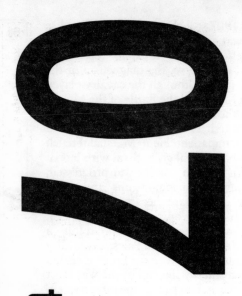

07

trench warfare

This chapter will cover:
- the need for a system of trenches
- the construction of the trench system
- everyday life in the trenches
- matters relating to morale and discipline
- the care of the wounded
- soldiers at rest away from the front.

'The firing trench is our place of business – our office in the city, so to speak. The supporting trench is our suburban residence where the weary toiler may betake himself periodically (or, more correctly, in relays) for purposes of refreshment and repose.'

(From *The First Hundred Thousand* by Ian Hay, 1876–1952)

The need for trenches

Trenches and trench warfare were not new. Advances in the technology of warfare meant that as weapons acquired greater range, became automatic and increased their firepower, men had to dig into the ground in order to survive. Trenches had already been used during the Crimean War, the American Civil War, the Franco-Prussian War and the Boer Wars, and during the First World War trench warfare was not confined to the Western Front but occurred in every battle area. On the Western Front, months of stalemate allowed a network of trenches to develop which honeycombed the battle-scarred countryside from the North Sea to the Swiss frontier. The trenches may have provided shelter from bullets and shrapnel but they only allowed the most primitive living conditions and for tens of thousands of men, trench warfare became a way of life, even a subculture. On their arrival in France, men were sent for additional training at a base camp that was intended to prepare them for the realities of life at the front. One such training area was the notorious Bull Ring at Etaples, known to the soldiers as 'Eat Apples' it was later to be the scene of a major army mutiny. Then it was off to the front either by train or by completing a series of gruelling route marches. On the march, men burdened with rifles and full packs were expected to cover 30 kilometres (18.6 miles) a day with ten minutes of each hour allowed for rest and it was during these marches that soldiers sang the songs that were to become so famous – *It's A Long Way To Tipperary*, *Mademoiselle From Armentières* and *Pack Up Your Troubles In Your Old Kit Bag*. The versions sung by the soldiers were very much cruder than those that became popular at home.

Trenches and the trench system

Basically, a trench is an extended hole dug into the ground that is a little over two metres (6.5 feet) deep and a little less than two metres wide. Some of the earth that was removed when digging the trench was used to create a parapet to the front that increased its height to nearly three metres (9.8 feet) whilst the remainder was piled to form an earthwork at the rear, a parados. The sides of the trench were reinforced with sandbags intended to absorb the impact of bullets and shrapnel. Trenches were not dug in straight lines but in irregular sections known as firebays and traverses that, from the air, resembled the battlements of a castle. The line of trenches closest to the enemy was known as the front line and behind this was a vast warren-like network of support and reserve trenches connected by communication trenches. Running forward from the front line towards the enemy, narrow and much shallower trenches were dug which were known as saps. Soldiers used these to crawl forward and observe the enemy's movements more closely. Within each trench there was a ledge or firestep on which men stood to see and fire over the top. Another feature of the trenches was the dugouts – these were shelters scooped out of the back of the trenches to provide the crudest living accommodation. The front of a dugout might be no more than an overhanging groundsheet that allowed minimum privacy and barely any shelter from the elements. The floor of the trench was lined with planking – duckboards that allowed soldiers to move more easily in the mud. The area separating the two opposed front lines was known as 'no man's land' and whilst the distance between them varied, in places it was 50 metres (164 feet) or less. At one point near La Boisselle on the Somme, it was claimed that the trenches were close enough for the British and Germans to shake hands over the top! Apart from the towns such as Etaples ('Eat Apples') Poperinge ('Pop'), Ypres ('Wipers'), soldiers also gave trenches, local woods and other landmarks nicknames – Blighty Wood, Crucifix Corner, Death Valley, Devil's Wood (Delville Wood), Hawthorn Ridge, Mucky Farm (Mouquet Farm), Owl Trench and Sanctuary Wood.

The cattle ranchers on the Great Plains of North America were the first to use barbed wire. On the Western Front, barbed-wire entanglements were used to guard the approaches to front-line trenches and for obvious reasons the barbed wire had to be pitched at least a grenade's throw away. Erecting and repairing the barbed wire was a dangerous business that was usually done at night using padded mallets or corkscrew-like supports that did not have to be hammered into the ground and so possibly alert the enemy.

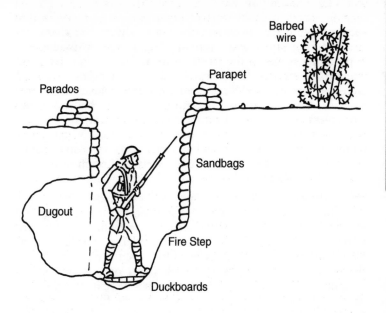

figure 13 a cross section of a trench

Life in the trenches

Once at the front, new arrivals would be 'shown the ropes' by 'old sweats', the men already well experienced in the daily routine that was trench life. It would be very wrong to assume that life in the front line was always hectic with constant attacks and counterattacks since the amount of activity varied and there were times when soldiers went for weeks without being involved in any action. Men were divided into watches and allocated duties and most of their day was spent engaged in boring routine that included rifle inspections, repairing trenches, digging latrines and other fatigues. They also enjoyed rest time when they could eat, sleep and write letters home. Even so, there was always a need to be on the alert against enemy-raiding parties and snipers. The critical periods of the day when the enemy was most likely to attack were at dawn and dusk and at these times, men had to 'stand to'. Darkness added to the need for caution and sentries were posted to keep watch across no man's land and report any movement. Men were also liable to be called upon to take part in night patrols to see what the enemy was up to. Of course, there was always the chance of encountering an enemy patrol. Night also provided an opportunity to repair the barbed wire and search for dead and wounded comrades. When star shells or Verey lights were fired high into the sky they illuminated the whole landscape and this was the time when men in no man's land had to stand motionless since the slightest movement was likely to attract a burst of machine-gun fire. 'Going over the top' as part of a raiding party or worse, to take part in a major offensive against the enemy demanded exceptional bravery and often resulted in a heavy loss of life.

In the trenches, maintaining any level of personal cleanliness was fraught with difficulties. Water, both for drinking and washing, was in short supply since it had to be brought forward from the rear and when water was available, men used their steel helmets as wash basins but often even a daily wash and shave was impossible. Baths were luxuries only to be enjoyed once out of the line. Lavatories or latrines were dug at the edge of the trenches and once full, they had to be filled in and new ones prepared. This work was the most disliked punishment imposed on soldiers for minor offences. The trenches were the breeding ground of millions of rats and other vermin that thrived on the scraps of food, litter, excrement and the remains of decomposing bodies. The loathsome creatures grew to an enormous size and became sufficiently bold to attack men whilst they were sleeping. They were also responsible for the contamination of food and the spread of disease. Men found ingenious ways of trapping and killing them although there were instances when they were kept as pets. Lice and fleas were other scourges of the trenches that infested men's hair and clothing and caused great discomfort. Some relief was to be found by cutting one's hair short or shaving it off altogether and men tried to rid their clothing of lice and fleas by running the seams of their underclothing over the flames of candles. Lice also caused a condition known as trench fever and infected soldiers needed up to 12 weeks to recover. In the summer, swarms of flies infested the trenches and dugouts where, like the rats, they fed on the dead and decomposing bodies that were riddled with their eggs and maggots. From the onset of autumn until late spring when the rainfall was at its highest, the trenches were filled with water and the landscape around became a morass of clinging mud. Although the trenches were lined with duckboards and the men had waterproof groundsheets and thigh-length gum boots to protect them against the ooze, many suffered from a form of foot rot known as trench foot. The usual remedy was the regular application of grease made from strong-smelling whale oil. Even more serious was frostbite that was the result of exposure to extreme cold and could lead to gangrene and even the need to amputate the affected limbs. To reduce the chances of soldiers suffering from these ailments, officers carried out regular foot inspections.

Food-wise, a British soldier was supposed to receive 4,193 calories a day. In practice, his daily ration depended on circumstances and therefore varied in quality and quantity with bully beef, akin to present day corned beef, biscuits and jam, almost invariably plum and apple, the common foods most readily available. Hot meals that included meat and vegetables were supplied by field kitchens and then sent forward to the men in the trenches but by the time it reached them it was often cold and unappetizing. Although it was officially forbidden, soldiers devised their own means of heating food by using a 'Tommy Cooker' which was a small, pocket-size stove fuelled by solidified alcohol that gave off some heat. Even so, there were sometimes long periods when men went without food of any sort. Every soldier carried with him iron rations which was dehydrated food that could only be used in a dire emergency and with the permission of an officer. All drinking water was chlorinated which made it safe but foul tasting. Dire and even fatal consequences resulted when men were tempted to drink from the polluted water found in craters.

Morale in the army varied from unit to unit and depended on such factors as the progress of the war, news from home, local conditions, casualty levels, the quality of the officers and the level of *esprit de corps*. Of necessity, discipline had to be strict. Lesser misdeeds were dealt with on the spot and punished by stoppages of pay and the imposition of additional duties and fatigues but for more serious offences, men were court-martialled. During the course of the war some 169,000 men were tried for offences ranging from being drunk and insubordinate to striking an officer, falling asleep on duty, cowardice, desertion and even murder. With soldiers entitled to a quarter of a litre of rum weekly and with liquor freely available behind the lines, drunkenness was a problem and over 35,000 men were charged with this offence. Much hated was Field Punishment Number 1 which was known as 'crucifixion'.

It humiliated the unfortunate offender by tying him to a fixed object for a number of hours each day in full view of his comrades. Although some 3,342 men were tried for crimes that merited the death sentence, only 343 were actually shot at dawn.

During the course of the war, the total number of British casualties reached some 2.69 million of which about a quarter were killed and over half the British soldiers involved in the war suffered a wound of one sort or another. In action, it was forbidden for a soldier to stop to help a fallen comrade and each man carried with him an emergency dressing which he could use to attend to his own wound. Otherwise, he had to wait to be discovered by stretcher-bearers of which every company possessed four. Bullet wounds were usually clean cut and much easier to deal with than wounds by shrapnel that could cause ghastly mutilation. The wounded were first taken to a regimental aid post located in the reserve trenches where they would be seen by a medical officer who would dress their wounds and administer any needed pain killers, usually injections of morphine. Next they would be moved to an Advanced Dressing Station where emergency surgery might be attempted and then on to a Casualty Clearing Station where teams of doctors were able to provide a wide range of more advanced treatment. The most seriously wounded would then be transferred to hospital by mobile ambulances or ambulance trains where they would be able to enjoy the long forgotten luxuries of clean sheets and good food. Doctors and nurses had to deal with the most appalling injuries which might require amputation and lead to disfigurement and cope with those suffering from gas blindness and shell shock. The symptoms of shell shock, a nervous disorder brought about by battle fatigue, were a vacant expression, ready smile and nervous facial twitch. Some medical officers refused to recognize the condition and considered such men to be malingerers. Have no doubt, there were those soldiers who 'tried it on' and would have been delighted to receive a 'blighty one' – a wound that was not life threatening but severe enough for them to be sent home. Injured soldiers were awarded a wound stripe and once they had recovered, sent back to the trenches. The dead were usually buried close to where they fell but in the heat of battle this was sometimes impossible and so bodies were interred in the bottom of the trench. Cemeteries were often established close to Casualty Clearing Stations but the problem was that the land was liable to be fought over time and time again so that exploding shells might disturb the ground and the location of the graves be lost forever. Not surprisingly, some of the dead were too badly decomposed or mutilated to be recognized and 160,000 British soldiers killed in the war have no known graves. To this day, building contractors in France and Belgium often unearth human remains that are still buried with full military honours.

In matters of religion, soldiers received guidance from army chaplains and padres. A chaplain's life was taken up with a range of emotive tasks – comforting the dying, taking down messages intended for next-of-kin, attending burials, consoling those at the end of their tether and being present at executions. Whenever it was possible, chaplains organized church services, known as drumhead services because the makeshift altar was often made of drums. Often Roman Catholic chaplains were called upon to go into the front line to administer last rites to the dying. Geoffrey Studdart-Kennedy, a much beloved Anglican clergyman, went into the trenches even when they were under enemy fire and handed out cigarettes to the troops. Nicknamed 'Woodbine Willy', his bravery earned him the Military Cross and he later became chaplain to King George V. At his funeral in 1929, old soldiers placed packets of Woodbines on his coffin as a mark of their respect and gratitude. At Poperinge in Belgium, 'Pop' to British soldiers, Colonel Reginald Talbot appointed a clergyman, Philips Clayton, to turn a house into a rest and recreation centre. 'Tubby' Clayton, as he became known, called the building Talbot House. In army signal jargon, it became known as Toc H and it was the first branch of an organization that was to spread worldwide. The original Toc H house in Poperinge remains open to visitors to this day.

Away from the front

The length of time a soldier spent in the front line varied according to circumstances. A typical arrangement would be for a man to spend four days in the front line, four in a support trench, eight in reserve and then enjoy a period of rest behind the lines but there were occasions when men spent 30 days and even longer in the front line without relief. Serving men looked forward to their annual leave of ten days, which included the time taken to reach home and return to his unit. Again, it was not uncommon for men to go much longer without seeing their families and there were instances when men on home leave committed suicide rather than return to the trenches. Letters from home were always most welcome as were parcels containing knitted gloves and scarves, chocolate, home-made delicacies and of course cigarettes. The troops loved their 'fags', which were often their only comfort in their otherwise miserable existence in the trenches. Sadly, not all the letters brought welcome news since some included news of a family bereavement or details of a wife's infidelity, a 'Dear John' letter. Such letters added to a soldier's discomfort and misery and might make him apply for compassionate leave.

Once at rest behind the front line, the first thing a soldier wanted was a wash, shave, change of clothes and sleep before they went in search of relaxation. Concert parties, film shows and sports events were organized for soldiers and the Young Men's Christian Association (YMCA) and other voluntary organizations ran canteens that provided tea and refreshments. Unfortunately not all the forms of relaxation they sought were that wholesome. With some soldiers gambling became an obsession and many lost their money playing 'Brag' whilst others preferred dice or Crown and Anchor. Many made their way to the *estaminets* in local towns and villages and there drank themselves senseless on beer and cheap wine. Others went off in search of brothels, *maisons de tolérance* as they were known, which sported the traditional red light and were uniform in their seediness. Even so, men queued at the door for their few minutes of pleasure and it was not surprising that venereal disease became a major problem. During the war there were over 150,000 reported cases of syphilis amongst British soldiers and those with VD were treated at a special hospital set aside for the purpose. The disgrace of 'having caught a dose' and penalties such as stoppages of pay and the cancellation of leave did little to reduce the number of cases. Occasionally units taken out of the line were not sent for rest but to camps where they were subject to drills, excessive 'bull' (spit and polish) and additional military training. As you can imagine, this was most unpopular and contributed to a number of army mutinies including one at Etaples in 1917.

Life in the trenches was harsh and brutal particularly for men who a few months earlier had been in civilian employment and had enjoyed quiet family lives. Even so, they were able to forge a sense of camaraderie that would help them share the dangers and suffering they were forced to endure with fortitude and unbelievable courage.

The language of the trenches – everyday words and phrases used by British soldiers

blighty	home
blighty wound	a wound serious enough for a a soldier to be sent home
bully beef	tinned beef like corned beef
Canary	a drill instructor
chit	a written message
crump	an exploding shell
'Digger'	an Australian soldier
dixie	a food container
'Doughboy'	an American soldier
duckboard	a board used to line the bottom of a trench
egg	a hand grenade
estaminet	a bar, a place where soldiers went to relax
fags	cigarettes, usually Woodbines
fatigues	duties sometimes given as a punishment
fleabag	a sleeping bag
'Fritz'	a German
'Froggies'	Frenchmen
funk hole	a place to shelter
going over the top	moving forward from the trenches
Hun	a German
iron rations	packs of emergency food
Maconochie	tinned food known by the manufacturer's name
maisons de tolérance	brothels
minenwerfter	a large German shell also known as a 'Moaning Minnie'

no man's land	the land between the opposed lines of trenches
pavé	a French cobbled road
phutt	to go phutt – to stop working
Plug Street	Ploegsteert, a Belgian town
Pop	Poperinge, a Belgian town
pork and beans	Portuguese soldiers
Red Cap	a military policeman
san fairy ann	from the French '*Ce ne fait rien*' – it doesn't matter
sapper	an engineer
shell shock	a nervous condition brought about by proximity to exploding shells
stand to	waiting in readiness for an enemy attack
Toc H	Talbot House
Tommy	a British soldier
Top Brass	senior officers
trench fever	a fever that affected men in the trenches carried by lice
trench foot	a condition of the feet arising from exposure to wet and cold
whizzbangs	German shells
Wipers	Ypres, a Belgian town
Yank	an American soldier

08

issues of bravery and cowardice

This chapter will cover:
- the award of medals and how acts of bravery were recognized
- some men who won the highest award for bravery – the Victoria Cross
- courts martial
- some men who were shot at dawn
- mutinies in the British army.

'Courage is willpower, whereof no man has an unlimited stock and, when in war it is used up, he is finished. A man's courage is his capital and he is always spending.'

(Lord Moran of Manton, 1882–1977, *The Anatomy of Courage*, 1945)

Reaction to fear

During the First World War there was ample evidence of the courage shown by men of all ranks and social backgrounds. Altogether 633 Victoria Crosses (VCs) and a great many other medals for gallantry were awarded to men serving in the armed forces of Britain and the Dominions. Of the VCs, 187 were awarded posthumously since, as was often the case, men found themselves in extreme situations where acts of bravery were needed to save the day and there were heroic men prepared to sacrifice their lives in order to save their comrades. Many headstones in British military cemeteries in France carry the biblical inscription 'Greater love hath no man than this, that a man lay down his life for a friend'. Of course, there were also those whose bravery was born of boldness and indifference to their own safety. On the other hand, 3,342 men were sentenced to death for a range of crimes that included cowardice and desertion. In a great many cases they had done their best but, as Lord Moran (later to become Winston Churchill's own personal physician) says, simply ran out of their stock of courage. Many of those sent for trial by courts martial fell victims of flawed judgements and miscarriages of justice.

Acknowledging acts of bravery

Servicemen receive medals for long service, good conduct and for being involved in a particular war or campaign. However, the most prestigious medals are those awarded for bravery. The few that are awarded the same medal twice receive a clasp or 'bar' to their original medal. Soldiers who served in the early stages of the First World War became eligible to receive the 1914 Star, sometimes called the Mons Star, as well as the 1914–15 Star. At the end of the war, all servicemen were awarded the British War and Victory Medals. A Star, War and Victory Medals were collectively nicknamed 'Pip, Squeak and Wilfred' whilst the War and Victory Medals alone were referred to as 'Mutt and Jeff' after two popular cartoon characters.

The highest award for gallantry was the Victoria Cross. This decoration which bears the inscription 'For Valour' and is only awarded to those who perform outstanding acts of bravery in battle, was founded by Queen Victoria during the Crimean War and was made from the metal of Russian guns captured during the siege of Sevastopol. During the war, one officer, Captain Noel Chavasse, an officer in the Royal Army Medical Corps (RAMC), twice won the medal in France in 1916 and again in Belgium in 1917. The Distinguished Service Order (DSO) was awarded to officers for meritorious service in time of war. Another medal awarded for bravery made only to officers was the Military Cross (MC) and over 37,000 were awarded during the war and of these 2,992 gained a bar, 116 a second bar and four a third bar. The similar award to other ranks was the Military Medal (MM) of which 121,554 were awarded. The Distinguished Conduct Medal (DCM) was also awarded for bravery in battle as well as a wide range of medals made available to servicemen from the Dominions.

Medals awarded to British and dominion servicemen 1914–18

Victoria Cross (VC)	633
Distinguished Service Order (DSO)	8,981
Military Cross	40,236
Military Medal	121,554
Distinguished Conduct Medal	24,591
Mons Star	365,622
1914–15 Star	2,078,183
British War Medal	6,610,000
Victory Medal	5,725,000

Battlefield commanders and commanders of ships at sea sent dispatches home for the attention of those in higher authority and in them it became the practice to mention by name those who had made some significant contribution to the success of any action. It was a lower grade of recognition and brought no award and it has been calculated that 2 per cent of all servicemen were 'mentioned in dispatches'. For British consumption, details of all awards appeared in the *London Gazette*, an official newspaper that also listed the names of men who had been commissioned. Amongst French awards for bravery were the *Légion d'honneur*, the *Medaille Militarie* and the *Croix de Guerre* whilst German servicemen received the

Eiserne Kreuz, the Iron Cross. This long-established medal dated back to 1813 and was awarded at two levels – First and Second Class.

Examples of men whose bravery earned them the Victoria Cross

Corporal Cecil Noble and Company Sergeant Major Harry Daniels

From Bournemouth in Dorset, England, Cecil Noble was a corporal serving with the Rifle Brigade. In March 1915 at Neuve Chapelle, France, German machine-gun fire and barbed wire entanglements held up the advance of his battalion and together with Company Sergeant Major Harry Daniels, he went forward and succeeded in cutting the wire. Both men were wounded and Noble later died of his injuries but Daniels survived and was later promoted to the rank of lieutenant-colonel. He died in Leeds in 1953.

Able Seaman William Williams

From Stanton Lacy, Shropshire, England, William Williams was a member of the crew of HMS *River Clyde*. In April 1915 at Cape Helles, Gallipoli, standing chest deep in the sea and under continuous Turkish fire, he held on to a rope that was securing smaller ships alongside. Severely wounded, he was killed by a shell whilst efforts were being made to rescue him. He was, said his commanding officer, 'the bravest sailor I have ever met'.

Private William McFadzean

Twenty-one-year-old Private McFadzean came from Lurgan, County Armagh and served in the Royal Irish Rifles. In July 1916 at Thiepval Wood, he was in a trench crowded with men when the safety pins fell out of two grenades. He immediately threw himself on top of the grenades that exploded and killed him instantly. By showing immense heroism, the young soldier gave his life in order to save his comrades.

Captain Noel Chavasse

Son of the Bishop of Liverpool, Noel Chavasse was a doctor attached to The King's Liverpool Regiment. In August 1916, he ignored heavy enemy fire to tend wounded men in no man's land and his bravery earned him the Victoria Cross. The following year at Wieltje in Belgium, although badly wounded himself, he refused to leave the front line and went in search of wounded men. He later died of his wounds and for his courage was awarded a second Victoria Cross.

Private Thomas Cooke

A New Zealander serving with the Australian Imperial Force, Thomas Cooke was awarded the Victoria Cross for his bravery at Pozières in September 1916. After a Lewis gun had been disabled, he was ordered to take his own gun to a dangerous part of the line where he soon came under heavy enemy fire. The only man left, he stuck to his post, continued firing and was later found dead beside his gun.

Sergeant Robert Bye

A sergeant in the Welsh Guards, Robert Bye came from Abercynon in South Wales. In July 1917, during an attack on German positions near the Yser Canal in Belgium, he noticed the havoc being caused by two German block-houses. He rushed at one and put it out of action before leading his men against the other. In accomplishing this, he killed 70 of the enemy and took many prisoners. Bye lived until 1962 when he died in Nottingham.

'Shot at dawn'

Under British Military Law there were numerous offences for which a serving soldier might be charged and if found guilty, face the death penalty. They included desertion, cowardice, mutiny, murder, quitting post, disobedience, striking a superior officer, sleeping on post and casting away arms. During the course of the war 348 men and three officers suffered this fate and of these some 268 were found guilty of desertion.

Executions of British and Dominion servicemen 1914–18

Desertion	268
Murder	37
Cowardice	18
Quitting post	7
Disobedience	5
Striking an officer	5
Mutiny	4
Sleeping on post	2
Casting away arms	2

There were four types of courts martial. A Regimental Court Martial dealt with relatively minor offences and the maximum penalty it could impose was 42 days' detention but more serious cases were considered by a District Court Martial that had the power to sentence a man to two years of hard labour, reduce him to the ranks or discharge him with ignominy. A General Court Martial which in wartime, of necessity, became a Field General Court Martial, sat to consider the most serious cases and could impose the death sentence. A man accused of an offence that carried the death penalty would be kept under close arrest until the time of his trial. The soldier involved would be offered the services of an officer to act as his defence council but the officer, known as the 'prisoner's friend', would be unlikely to have had any legal training. Sometimes soldiers chose to defend themselves but this was not a good idea since the man might only be of limited education and unable to express himself adequately. Before his trial one soldier wrote home to his mother, '... I'm in a bit of trouble now and won't get any money for a long time. I will have to go in front of a court. I will try my best to get out of it, so don't worry'. He was shot.

At such a court martial, the soldier or his representative, the 'prisoner's friend', had the right to call witnesses and cross-examine them and if the case could not be proved, the soldier was released immediately. If found guilty, the soldier might be sent to serve a period at an army detention centre with or without hard labour but if guilty of a capital crime, he would be sentenced to death. The sentence would not be carried out until the papers dealing with the case had been sent first to the man's battalion commander and then his brigade, division and corps commanders for them to add a recommendation. The papers would then reach the commander-in-chief for him to make a final decision.

A matter of justice?

The final decision as to whether a man should have his sentence commuted and live or confirmed and face the firing squad depended on a range of considerations – the soldier's previous record, details of his medical condition and any recommendations for mercy. The weight given to a soldier's previous record varied and some men with exemplary records were executed as were a few that had earlier been awarded medals for gallantry. Medical officers had varying views about possible extenuating circumstances such as the state of the man's health. They also disagreed about the impact of psychological factors – the effects of a long period in the front line and whether or not the soldier was suffering from shell shock. A commanding officer's concern at a decline in morale and the fighting spirit of his men might lead him to support the decision to execute a man simply *'pour encourager les autres'* – to encourage the others. Field Marshal Haig, himself, commented 'Moral fibre ... men who possess little or none of this would give way at the moment of stress were it not for the makeweight of the daily fear of punishment'. It is claimed that at one stage of the war there was unrest in the ranks because no officer had faced the firing squad and that this caused Haig to ensure that an officer charged would be shot. It should be noted that 40 per cent of the men executed had been volunteers who had enlisted at the outbreak of war and that they had offered to fight for their country but once at the front, had been unable to cope with the rigours of war. There were occasions when court martial procedures were not followed and some where they were totally ignored. It should also be remembered that only a small minority of soldiers found guilty of a capital crime were actually shot – 343 out of 3,080, just 11 per cent. Of those executed, two thirds had previously been convicted of a breach of military law and 37 were murderers when the sentence would have been mandatory. There were instances when men shot their own comrades in drunken brawls; one man shot a fellow soldier after he had discovered that he had not fairly distributed the loot after they had jointly burgled a house; two others conspired to shoot their unpopular sergeant-major and shot the wrong man!

Executions

The first execution took place on 8 September 1914 just four weeks after the war started when Private Thomas Highgate, who was just 19 years old was shot for desertion. During the course of the war 13 gunners of the Royal Artillery were executed, 12 men from the West Yorkshire Regiment and five men from the same battalion of the Worcestershire Regiment were shot on the same day. Executions took place at dawn and were usually carried out by a firing squad drawn from the man's own battalion. It was an unpopular task and selected men were known to plead not to be included and it was said that 'self-respecting soldiers ... screamed out begging not to be made into murderers'. After writing his last letter home and spending some time with the chaplain, the unfortunate man, probably bolstered with rum, would be taken to the place of execution where he would be formally identified, blindfolded and his hands fastened behind him. Tied to a post or made to sit in a chair, a square of white material would be placed over his heart to serve as a target for the firing party. No point would be served in aiming off since, if there were still signs of life after the volley had been fired, the officer in charge had to deliver a *coup de grace* with his own revolver. At the start of the war, the soldier's family was informed of the soldier's disgrace and any allowance paid to his wife and children stopped but Haig reversed this so that the family was not informed, the allowance continued to be paid and the soldier buried amongst other fallen comrades. In spite of considerable pressure, the Australian authorities refused to allow the death penalty to be applied to their soldiers. Although estimated at only 48, the Germans have never made known their figures, but they did express surprise at the number executed by the British. Although records indicate that only 133 Frenchmen suffered the death penalty there is reason to believe there may have been many more following army mutinies in 1917.

Some famous cases

Private Albert Ingham

Before the war, Albert Ingham had worked as a clerk for the Lancashire and Yorkshire Railways. In 1914, he was amongst the first to volunteer and joined the Manchester Regiment. After serving in Egypt, he arrived on the Western Front and survived the Battle of the Somme. By October 1916, he had endured enough and together with a friend, Alfred Longshaw, he deserted. The two men reached Dieppe and managed to get on board a Swedish ship before being discovered and handed over to the Military Police. At their court martial, both men were sentenced to death and in spite of efforts to save the doomed men, they were both executed on 1 December 1916. Ingham's father was told that his son had died of wounds and when he discovered the truth, he asked that his son's headstone carry the inscription 'Murdered by the British army'. This was refused but it was agreed that it could read 'Shot at dawn. One of the first to enlist. A worthy son of his father.' The inscription is unique since it is the only headstone to indicate the true cause of death of an executed soldier.

Sub-Lieutenant Edwin Dyett

At the start of the war, Cardiff-born Edwin Dyett, the 19-year-old son of a merchant navy captain and the brother of a serving naval officer, volunteered to join the Royal Navy. Unfortunately, a surplus of sailors meant that many were transferred to serve in the Royal Naval Division which meant that they effectively became soldiers. Dyett, a sub-lieutenant in the Nelson Battalion, was sent to serve in the trenches on the Western Front. A nervous young man and quite unsuited to soldiering, Dyett was recognized as an inferior officer and kept in reserve but unfortunately the high casualty rate made it necessary for him to be sent to the front line. On 13 November 1916, in the confusion of battle, Dyett got lost and instead of following orders, attempted to make his own way back to his lines and ended up sheltering in a shell crater. Most officers found unsuitable for trench warfare were sent home and given a desk job but this was not to happen in the case of Dyett. Charged with desertion, he was found guilty and sentenced to death. There were said to have been irregularities about his trial and much of the evidence against him came from an officer who bore him a grudge. When giving evidence himself, Dyett did not mention his family's naval connections or the fact that he was distantly related to Field Marshal Sir John French. Everyone assumed that his sentence would be commuted but on 5 January 1917, he was shot. It has since been claimed that because soldier–sailor relations were not good, Dyett was a scapegoat and his execution a political gesture. On hearing the news, his father emigrated overseas and swore never again to set foot in Britain.

Private George Everill

Private George Everill of the North Staffordshire Regiment must have had one of the worst military records in the British army. Originally a placid and well-behaved soldier, in March 1916 he faced his first charge of insubordination and was sentenced to one year's imprisonment with hard labour but the sentence was suspended. Five weeks later, he was charged with wilful defiance and was sentenced to ten years' penal servitude but once again his sentence was commuted to only two years. In March 1917, Private Everill was charged with being absent and his one year sentence was commuted to 90 days' Field Punishment Number 1. Shortly after his release he was charged with using threatening language to a superior officer and again his three year sentence was commuted to 90 days. After serving his time, he was charged with showing wilful defiance. At his court martial he declined to question witnesses and, not surprisingly, no evidence was produced of his previous good conduct. This time he had gone too far and was sentenced to death and after Haig had confirmed the sentence, the 30-year-old soldier finally faced the firing squad at Poperinge on 14 September 1917. His wife, who believed that her husband had been killed in action, saw to it that the epitaph on his grave read, 'Thy will be done from his loving wife and children'.

Mutinies

The reaction of some soldiers to the horrors of trench warfare was not limited to trying to get away from it all by deserting and there were incidents of open mutiny by individual soldiers as well as whole units of men. In May 1915, a battalion of the Welsh Regiment undergoing training at home registered their disgust at the bullying of their NCOs, largely drawn from the Guards and the Metropolitan Police, by refusing to obey orders. An attempt at intimidation failed and the military authorities were forced to back down. Later the same year, men from the same regiment again refused to obey orders this time to show their opposition to Field Punishment Number 1, 'crucifixion'. Far more serious was the mutiny that occurred in the military prison at Blargies near Rouen. On this occasion many of the 300 men held in the prison openly protested at the excessive punishments, the poor food and the fact that there were only 14 latrines with each man allocated a daily usage of 45 seconds. When some men resisted being put in leg irons, order had to be restored through the use of armed force. As a result of the courts martial that followed, two men were executed – an Englishman and a New Zealander – but the other ringleaders, being Australians, avoided the death penalty. By far the largest mutiny of the war occurred at Etaples in September 1917.

The Etaples mutiny

Etaples, close to Le Touquet and on the estuary of the River Canche, was a military base at which soldiers received further military training before proceeding to the front line. At the base there were also hospitals and convalescent homes, various facilities for relaxation and a detention camp for offenders. The regime at the base was harsh and the conditions spartan and at the much hated 'Bull Ring', a parade ground on the sand dunes, men were drilled and bullied by instructors known as 'Canaries' because of their yellow arm bands, and the 'Red Caps', the Military Police. To make matters worse, soldiers on leave from the front were sometimes made to drill like new recruits. The situation came to a head in September 1917 when a riot broke out and soldiers ignored sentries and tried to enter the town of Etaples. The base commander's office was broken into and Brigadier-General Thompson himself manhandled. Officers were insulted and one soldier was heard to shout 'Don't listen to the bloody officer. What you want to do is tie a rope round his neck'. With men brandishing red flags and reports of rape and looting in the town, the situation was getting out of hand and troops from the Honourable Artillery Company had to be sent to Etaples to restore order. During the episode, one man was killed and afterwards, another soldier was charged with mutiny and executed.

In 1986, the events of the Etaples mutiny were the subject of a BBC series, *The Monocled Mutineer*, based on a book of the same name by William Allison and John Fairley. The central character of the series was a dashing rogue and anti-hero figure, Percy Toplis, a private in the Royal Army Medical Corps, who, so it was claimed, was one of the ringleaders of the mutiny. Toplis undoubtedly existed and the BBC series claimed that he often masqueraded as an officer and brazenly attended officers' mess functions wearing a monocle. However, subsequent research failed to prove that Toplis was ever at Etaples. After the war Toplis was wanted by the police and finally died in a shoot-out on a country road in the north of England. There were also other riots and mutinies and late in 1917 Chinese and Egyptians employed by the British army in Labour Corps went on strike. Although unarmed, they were fired on and many were killed and wounded. In July 1918, there was further trouble amongst British soldiers at a base near Calais and although the situation turned ugly, it did not develop to match the events at Etaples the previous year.

09

1916 – Verdun and the Somme

This chapter will cover:

- the general situation on the Western Front in 1916
- the significance of the Battle of Verdun
- the reasons for the change at the top when Haig replaced French
- the significance of the Battle of the Somme
- the consequences of both these battles and the situation at the end of the year.

'Where have all the soldiers gone?
   Long time passing.
Where have all the soldiers gone?
   Long time ago.
Where have all the soldiers gone?
   They've gone to graveyards every one,
When will they ever learn?
   When will they ever learn?'

(From a song, *Where Have All the Flowers Gone*,
by the American protest singer, Pete Seeger, 1919–)

The situation on the Western Front at the start of 1916

The last months of 1915 had been relatively quiet on the Western Front. It was a period during which both sides considered their options and planned their strategy for 1916. The German High Command was fully aware that it did not

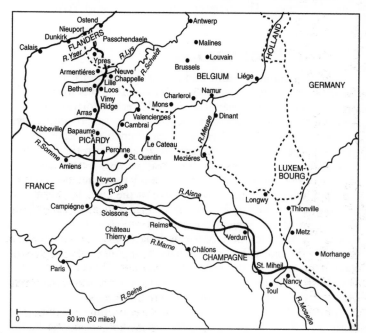

figure 14 Verdun and the Somme – the offensives of 1916

have the manpower or material resources of the Allies and feared the consequences of continuing to fight an indefinite war of attrition. Some thought was given to offensives against Russia and Italy but Erich von Falkenhayn, the German Commander-in-Chief, considered the Russians to already be beaten and was content to leave the Austrians to cope on the Italian Front. The offensive when it came was to be on the Western Front, but where?

By this stage of the war, the Germans had identified Britain as being their major enemy and thought their best ploy was to 'knock her best sword ... out of her hand'. Strangely, the Germans considered the 'best sword' of the British to be the French army and Erich von Falkenhayn sent a memorandum to the Kaiser:

> 'There are objectives within our reach ... for which the French General Staff would be forced to throw in every man they have. If they do so, the forces of France will be bled to death, since there can be no question of voluntary withdrawal ... The objectives of which I speak are Belfort and Verdun ... The preference must be given to Verdun.'

The Battle of Verdun

Verdun – the name is Gallic and means 'powerful fortress' – is a city that lies on the banks of the River Meuse and is strategically based on the road between Rheims and Metz. A fortress city and important military base surrounded by a series of impressive fortresses, it was at the centre of the French defensive system and was the only garrison to effectively resist the invaders during the Franco-Prussian War. Falkenhayn knew that the capture of the city would be a major blow to French morale and that they would defend it irrespective of the cost. He estimated that the fall of the city would lead to a political crisis and the resignation of the French government and his immediate aim was to lay siege to the city for as long as he was able and to slaughter as many French soldiers as possible. Falkenhayn's code name for the offensive was *Gericht*, 'Execution place'. Verdun stood at the point where the front line crossed the River Meuse and the French authorities were of the opinion that a city surrounded by so many fortresses must be impregnable. The truth was that the fortresses were in a state of disrepair, the trench systems between them were inadequate and their heavy guns had been moved elsewhere.

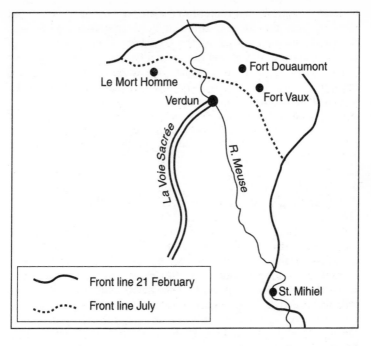

figure 15 the Battle of Verdun

After bad weather had caused the abandonment of the date
originally set for the attack, the German offensive finally began
on the morning of 21 February 1916. Before Falkenhayn's
troops moved forward, the French positions were subjected to a
nine-hour bombardment. Even so, their first attempt to break
through the line of fortresses failed and they made little progress
against strong French resistance. During the following days they
had only limited success until 25 February when Fort
Douaumont, the most important of the French fortresses, fell to
the Germans. The story of its capture is a mixture of disastrous
oversight by the French and remarkable good fortune by the
Germans. Some 200 metres (656 feet) long and 100 metres (328
feet) wide, the concrete mass of Fort Douaumont was protected
by barbed wire, spiked railings and a ditch whilst the
surrounding fortifications bristled with machine guns and gun
turrets. Yet, in spite of its impressive array of defences, it fell due
to the ingenuity of a German sergeant and his party of nine men.
Sergeant Kunze and his men took advantage of the fact that the
fortress was inadequately defended to reach the wall of the

fortress unnoticed and there they formed a human pyramid and climbed into the fortress through a narrow opening. Others followed and by the end of the day, Fort Douaumont was in German hands. That evening, the French appointed a new commander to lead the armies defending Verdun, Marshal Philippe Pétain. From a prosperous peasant family in the Pas-de-Calais, Pétain had only been a colonel in 1914 but promotion came quickly. His immediate task was to restore the morale of his men and famously declaring *'ils ne passeront pas'*, 'they shall not pass', he ordered a series of desperate counterattacks. The ability of the French to defend Verdun depended on reinforcements and supplies that reached the beleaguered city by way of one narrow road, *la Voie Sacrée*, the Sacred Way. Although under constant heavy German shellfire, during one critical week in February, over 25,000 tonnes of supplies and 190,000 men reached Verdun by means of the road. Later it was estimated that a vehicle passed along the road every 14 seconds and that in all, something like 60 per cent of the French army were to pass along it bound for 'the dreadful Calvary of Verdun'. Even though losses on both sides were appalling, the road ensured that the French garrison survived. The Germans next tried to take Fort Vaux but again it was stubbornly defended. During the struggle the French commander lost contact with his headquarters and an urgent request for support had to be sent by carrier pigeon. The brave bird delivered the message but then dropped dead. It was later awarded the *Légion d'honneur*. In spite of these efforts, Fort Vaux finally fell to the Germans. In an attempt to bring his offensive to a successful conclusion, Falkenhayn broadened his attacks but French resistance remained as determined as ever. As G. D. Sheffield has written, 'with all restraints cast to the wind, amid the shattered trenches and shellholes ceaselessly pounded by artillery, two mighty nations were locked in a struggle to the death' (*Leadership in the Trenches*, 2000). A pilot flying over Verdun noted that 'every sign of humanity had been swept away' and 'woods and roads have vanished like chalk wiped from a blackboard'. He concluded that the scene below reminded him of Dante's *Inferno*.

As Falkenhayn slowly came to realize the futility of it all, he tried to end the battle but his superiors insisted that it continue. Yet another German attempt to break through failed and to make things even more difficult, on 1 July the British had launched an offensive to the north close to the River Somme. During the first six months of the Battle of Verdun, Falkenhayn had failed to take the fortress city, lost 280,000 men and worse was to follow. In October, a French counterattack took the Germans completely by surprise and they were able to advance five kilometres (three miles), retake Fort Douaumont and Fort Vaux and capture 9,000 prisoners. Falkenhayn, who had set out to hammer and destroy the French army on 'the anvil of Verdun', had himself witnessed the slaughter of thousands of his men. In the end, the savagery of the ten-month battle resulted in 542,000 French and 434,000 German casualties. In a reshuffle at the top of the German High Command, Falkenhayn was dismissed and replaced by Hindenburg and Ludendorff whilst on the French side, their Commander-in-Chief, Marshal Joffre, gave way to Robert Nivelle.

Changes at the top – French replaced by Haig

At the end of 1915, Field Marshal Sir John Haig replaced Field Marshal Sir John French as commander-in-chief of the British armies on the Western Front. The two men were very different in character and outlook.

John Denton Pinkstone French was born in 1852. He had earlier taken part in the failed mission to rescue General Gordon in Khartoum and gained something of a good reputation during the Boer Wars since he had led the force that relieved Kimberley and for his exploits had been promoted to brigadier-general and received a knighthood. He was next appointed Chief of the Imperial General Staff and in 1913 was promoted to field marshal. In 1914, he took command of the BEF but soon doubts arose about his ability since he appeared to lack an understanding of the overall situation and was thought too indecisive. Some were also of the opinion that he had failed to make the best of the opportunities that arose. Views about him were mixed and he was described as being 'vain, ignorant and vindictive' whilst another general went as far as to consider him 'an ignorant little fool'. On the other hand, Kitchener admired him for 'his soldier-like qualities' and Winston Churchill considered him to be a 'natural soldier'. French was not helped by his womanizing that involved him in several scandals or by the fact that one of his sisters, Charlotte Despard, was a well-known pacifist, socialist, campaigner for women's rights and a supporter of Sinn Fein.

Douglas Haig was born in 1861 into a family of well-known Scotch whisky distillers. Like French, he was a cavalryman who had served in the Sudan and the Boer Wars and of significance was the fact that he was married to Dorothy Vivian, one of the queen's ladies-in-waiting. A deeply religious man, he was considered to be more liberal and forward looking than most other senior officers. In 1914, he went to France as commander of the British First Army and although his early conduct was undistinguished, his determined defence of Ypres enhanced his reputation. From the start, he had doubts concerning the suitability of French to command and made his views known to King George V in a series of secret communications. As we shall see, views about Haig were to become even more controversial than those about French.

Whatever his shortcomings, French had been quick to appreciate the inevitability of trench warfare and in a letter to the King wrote 'the spade will be as great a necessity as the rifle'. A year later he indicated his dislike of what was going on around him, 'War is really a brutal way of settling differences and the more I see of it, the more I hate it'. Haig, on the other hand, was intent on a war of attrition and in 1915, he commented, 'The enemy should never be given a complete rest by day or night, but be relentlessly worn down by exhaustion and loss until his defence collapses.' Finally, dissatisfaction with French's leadership coupled with behind-the-scenes intrigue that undermined his position led to his dismissal.

In June 1916, the Germans approached the French government with peace proposals. From the German viewpoint, the time seemed opportune since they thought the French were in difficulties following their heavy losses at Verdun and imagined they would be in a strong position to gain advantageous peace terms. The Allied leaders saw things very differently since with Verdun still in French hands and a new offensive being planned, they felt far from defeated and were in no mood to consider peace terms. They still wanted nothing other than out and out victory. Significantly, only those at the top knew of the German peace overtures and they saw no need to make them generally known in order to test the reaction of public opinion.

The Battle of the Somme

As early as December 1915, a conference of Allied leaders had met at Chantilly and had agreed to a joint offensive on the Western Front during the coming summer. Haig would have preferred to have waited until his troops had more combat experience and tanks had arrived at the front in sufficient numbers to have an impact. However, by spring the pressure on the French at Verdun had made the offensive an urgent necessity and plans were made for it to take place along a 28-kilometre (17-mile) front that ran from Gommecourt to a point just north of the River Ancre and then southwards below the high ground, Pozières Ridge, and on to the Somme Valley.

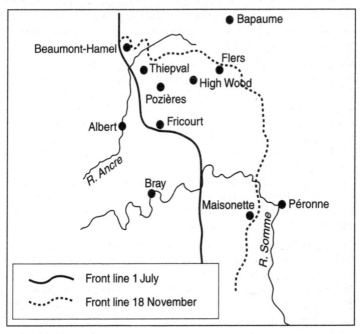

figure 16 the Somme battlefield

The major town immediately to the rear of the British lines was Albert. Always full of military, it was heavily bombarded and numerous shells hit the town's basilica surmounted by a statue of a golden Virgin and Child. The statue did not fall but hung precariously over the side at right angles to the ground where British engineers made it secure. There was a legend that the war would not end until the statue fell.

The line of advance was to stretch to the north and south of the main road between Albert and Bapaume with most of this line

covered by the British 4th Army under General Sir Henry
Rawlinson and the French 6th Army responsible for the
remainder. Although Haig was the Commander-in-Chief, he left
the detailed planning of the offensive to the man on the spot,
Rawlinson. Even so, there were sharp differences of opinion
between the two men since Haig wanted an all-out offensive
that would result in a major breakthrough; Rawlinson however
favoured a more gradual approach that would involve 'bite and
hold' operations – a series of offensives each with limited aims.
On paper, the plan produced by Rawlinson was simple enough.
The first stage of the battle would be a week-long bombardment
of the German lines which he supposed would virtually
eliminate any opposition before the infantry moved forward.
Rawlinson was of the opinion that since the majority of his men
were inexperienced civilian volunteers, to avoid any confusion it
would be best if they advanced towards the enemy in an orderly
fashion, line abreast. Their path through their own barbed wire
would be marked with white tape. Once the enemy line had
been broken, the cavalry would charge through into the open
ground beyond and outflank and roll up the enemy. The date for
the opening of the offensive was set for 1 July 1916. Although
Haig had concerns about certain aspects of Rawlinson's plan he
chose not to make them known.

The bombardment of the German trenches began on 24 June and
continued night and day for the next six days. At the same time,
tunnellers made final preparations to explode mines at various
points under the German front line to mark the start of the
assault. As the final hours passed, battalion commanders
emphasized that the attack next morning would be a walkover
and one commander went as far as to tell his men, 'When you go
over the top you can slope arms, light up your pipes and
cigarettes and march all the way to Pozières before seeing any
live Germans'. Another commented, 'Tomorrow, you will be able
to go over the top with a walking stick, you will not need a rifle'
but no one was more optimistic than Captain Nevill of the East
Surreys who provided each of his four platoons with footballs to
kick across no man's land and offered a prize for the first to kick
the ball into the enemy's trenches. Others were less sure. Whilst
on leave, Captain Martin of the Devonshire Regiment made a
model of the area of the front immediately ahead of his battalion
and on his return to France, used it to illustrate that when the
men went forward as suggested, German machine gunners on the
hill opposite would mow them down. His commanding officer
chose to discount his findings. Two days before the battle,

another officer in the same regiment, William Hodgson, wrote a prophetic poem, *Before Action*, that concluded:

'I, that on my familiar hill
   Saw with uncomprehending eyes
A hundred of Thy sunsets spill
   Their fresh and sanguine sacrifice,
'Ere the sun swings his noonday sword
   Must say goodbye to all of this:-
By all delights that I shall miss,
   Help me to die, O Lord.'

The first day of the Battle of the Somme was to be the blackest day in the history of the British army. In the British trenches, men, with bayonets fixed, and young officers, whistles in their mouths, waited for the last minutes to tick away. Then suddenly at 7.20 a.m. the mines at Hawthorn Ridge and La Boisselle were detonated and explosions sent huge columns of earth into the air. Then ten minutes later the guns fell silent and urged on by whistles and the encouragement of their platoon commanders, the infantrymen rose from their trenches, made their way through the barbed wire, formed lines and advanced forward. The men did not realize that the shelling had failed to destroy the enemy's barbed wire or that many of the shells, one estimate is a third, had not exploded. Even more significant was the fact that because German trenches and dugouts were dug deeper and better constructed than the British, many of their men had survived the bombardment. To the Germans, the end of the bombardment was a signal that the British attack was about to begin and they were quickly out of their dugouts and in position behind their machine guns. Even though a German counterbarrage began to rain shells on them, the British infantrymen came steadily on. Then the Germans began to blaze away at the sitting targets of rows of advancing soldiers. As the lines began to wither away, soon no man's land was piled high with the dead and the dying. John Giles has vividly described the scene as 'a slaughter yard, with wounded men screaming among the mutilated bodies of the dead' (*From Mons to the Marne*, 1977). As planned, Captain Nevill's company set off with their footballs towards the German lines but they didn't get far before the officer and his men were all killed in no man's land. Near Mametz, Captain Martin had also led his men forward and as his model had shown, they came immediately into full view of the enemy and, caught on an exposed slope, they were mown down. His body, together with another 159 men of the

Devonshires, was later buried in the trench from which they had emerged. Another to perish in the same place and at the same time was the poet Lieutenant Hodgson whose poem suggested that he had some premonition of his fate. In spite of the chaos and slaughter elsewhere, at the southern extremity of the line, the British and French gained some success and reached their objectives. This was largely because the men had moved forward into no man's land and then advanced towards the enemy behind a creeping barrage. Such a barrage moves just ahead of the advancing troops and forces the enemy to keep their heads down.

The historian A. J. P. Taylor (1954) wrote, 'Kitchener's army found its graveyard on the Somme'. On the first day alone, the British army suffered 57,470 casualties of which 19,240 were killed, 35,493 wounded and 2,152 missing and in addition the German also took 585 prisoners. In the close-knit communities in which some of the 'Pals Battalions' had been recruited, every street had families that mourned the loss of a husband, father, son or brother. The Accrington Pals suffered 585 casualties, the Leeds Pals 528 and the Bradford Pals 515. Some must have been mystified by the headlines in some British newspapers that were a travesty of the truth!

The first day of the Somme as reported in the British local newspaper, *The Southern Evening Echo*.

The first day of the battle – what went wrong?

At the start, Haig never really challenged Rawlinson over their different views regarding the tactics to be used in the planned offensive. Crucially, the heavy bombardment of the German positions failed in its aim since many shells failed to explode which meant that much of the German barbed wire was left intact. The superior construction of their defensive positions meant that many of the German troops survived and the sudden end to the bombardment provided the signal that the Allied offensive was about to start. The time lapse between the end of the bombardment and the advance of the infantrymen allowed the Germans to get into position to repel the attack. As the infantrymen made their way through the barbed wire along routes indicated by white tape, so they emerged at exit points that attracted the concentrated fire of German machine gunners. The British infantrymen were misled into believing the assault on the German positions would be a walkover and consequently, under instruction, they made their way forward in lines abreast and at a walking pace. They presented an easy target, as did the waves of infantry that followed them. Even worse, they found themselves floundering amongst their own dead and wounded.

The Somme – the slaughter continues

The carnage of 1 July and the failure to achieve a breakthrough did not deter the military command. In a battle that was to continue for the best part of five months, Rawlinson persisted with the same tactics so that each ridge and wood became the scene of a battle with a heavy loss of life. Positions were often taken, lost and then taken again. During the remainder of July, the 28th (Welsh) Division became involved in a costly struggle for Mametz Wood which cost the Welshmen 4,000 casualties whilst the 18th Division lost a further 4,000 men during a six-day battle to take nearby Trones Wood. It was left to the South African Brigade to drive the Germans from Delville Wood and of the 3,153 men that went into action only 773 emerged unscathed. Towards the end of the month, the Australians set out to capture Pozières Ridge and 8,000 lost their lives fighting for the important high ground. In August, it took three weeks of heavy fighting to capture the area around one farm, Mouquet

Farm, 'Mucky Farm' to the British soldiers, which was part of a German defensive line. The following month there was heavy fighting around Flers and it was here that tanks were used in battle for the first time. Of the 13 tanks that set out, 12 reached the German lines and, of these, six advanced as far as the village. Thiepval, one of the original objectives on 1 July, was finally taken on 25 September with both sides suffering terrible losses and it was here that the Ulster Division alone lost 4,000 men. A small wooded mound, the Butte de Warlencourt, beside the road leading to Bapaume was also the scene of bitter fighting. Fortified by the Germans so that it became honeycombed with tunnels, it changed hands time and time again and did not finally fall to the British until February 1917. The battle for the heights above the River Ancre began early in October and it lasted until the capture of Beaumont Hamel and Beaucourt in mid-November. These were the closing events in the Battle of the Somme.

The Somme – was it worth it?

In just over 20 weeks, at the furthest point the Allies had managed to advance 11 kilometres (seven miles). It had been a long and murderous slog that failed to achieve the desired breakthrough and during the course of the battle Allied casualties totalled 614,105 of which 419,654 were British and Dominion soldiers. The cost to the Germans was about 650,000 and a German staff officer later described the Somme as 'the muddy grave of the German field army'. Was the battle an Allied victory? If it was, it was a Pyrrhic victory and Haig must have wondered how many such victories he could afford. In truth, the loss of life affected the morale of the fighting men on both sides and at home, recruiting figures slumped so that the conscription of men had to be considered. No longer was joining the army regarded as the start of 'a great adventure'.

Postscript

Today, the legacy of the battle can still be found on the Somme. Shell cases, ammunition and barbed wire can be found and local farmers turn up what they refer to as their 'Iron Harvest'. They still represent a danger and can still cause fatalities. The battlefield also contains a great many military cemeteries and memorials to those that fell in the battle. The largest is the

Memorial to the Missing at Thiepval which is situated on a ridge and can be seen at a distance from various parts of the battlefield. Designed by Sir Edwin Lutyens, the panels on the central archway and numerous smaller arches list the names of the 73,412 men who died during 1916 and 1917 and have no known graves. At times, much of the Somme and other battlefields became a blaze of red poppies. Their appearance was due to the disturbance of land and the release of seeds caused by the digging of trenches, exploding shells and the burial of the dead. After the war, the former British commander-in-chief set up the Haig Fund to assist ex-servicemen. The Fund, now managed by the British Legion, adopted the poppy as a symbol of remembrance.

10

the war at sea

This chapter will cover:
- the comparative strengths of the British and German navies
- the early encounters in the North Sea
- the threat posed by German surface raiders
- the Battle of Jutland
- blockades and the nature of submarine warfare
- the methods used by the Allies to beat the submarine threat.

'Oh, dear, what comfort can I find?
 None this tide,
 Nor any tide,
Except he did not shame his kind –
Not even with the wind blowing, and that tide.'

(From *My Boy Jack*, a poem written
by Rudyard Kipling in honour of the
teenage hero of Jutland, John Cornwell)

The British and German navies – a comparison

Britain and Germany had begun their struggle to win naval supremacy long before the outbreak of the war. During the period between 1906 and 1915, Admiral Sir John Fisher brought about a revolution in naval construction with the introduction of the ironclad *Dreadnought* and Admiral Alfred von Tirpitz saw to it that Germany did not lag behind in the production of these new ships. Even so, Britain still retained the leadership in all types of vessels.

The British and German navies in 1914		
	Britain	Germany
Dreadnought-type battleships	20	13
Battlecruisers*	8	5
Cruisers	102	41
Destroyers	301	144
Submarines	78	30

*A battlecruiser was a ship with the guns of a battleship and the speed of a cruiser. To make this possible, its armour was lighter than that of a battleship and critics claimed that this made such ships vulnerable.

The greater part of the British Grand Fleet was based at Scapa Flow in the Orkney Islands and there were also other major naval bases at Rosyth, Chatham, Portsmouth and Plymouth. The German High Seas Fleet was located at Bremen, Cuxhaven, Emden, Kiel and Wilhelmshaven. In addition, both Britain and Germany had squadrons of warships scattered across the oceans of the world. The war started with a blow to British naval prestige when the German warships, *Goeben* and *Breslau*, outwitted their pursuers and made their way through the Mediterranean to reach Constantinople. Their success largely contributed to Turkey's decision to enter the war on Germany's side. Elsewhere in Europe, the German navy was content to raid towns along the British East Coast such as Lowestoft, Scarborough and Hartlepool. A major achievement of the Royal Navy during this time was the movement of the BEF across the English Channel to France without loss of life and it also managed to cut the German transatlantic undersea cable and so sever that country's links with North America.

Early North Sea encounters

First blood went to the Royal Navy when in August 1914 four German cruisers were sunk off Heligoland Bight but this was avenged the following month when a German submarine torpedoed three British cruisers with the loss of 1,600 lives. German hit-and-run raids along the British East Coast continued and one such raid caused over 500 civilian casualties but as British radio surveillance improved, so such raids became more hazardous and less frequent. Although the Royal Navy was more powerful than the German *Kriegsmarine*, neither side was keen to risk a major naval engagement that might involve heavy losses. So important was the Royal Navy to British war strategy that Winston Churchill, the First Lord of the Admiralty, said of the British naval Commander-in-Chief, Admiral John Jellicoe that he was 'the only man on either side who could lose the war in an afternoon'. The Royal Navy gained a major advantage when, unknown to the Germans, the Russians managed to obtain a copy of their code books and passed the details to the British. It was because of this that in January 1915, a German cruiser squadron was intercepted in the North Sea and at the Battle of the Dogger Bank, Admiral Beatty's ships drove the Germans off and succeeded in sinking the *Blucher* with the loss of 950 lives.

German surface raiders

Whilst the Royal Navy might have possessed the most powerful fleet in the word, it could not always guarantee the safety of British merchant shipping across the world's oceans. Most troublesome were the activities of German surface raiders that were active along shipping lanes in the Pacific and Indian

Oceans as well as the Caribbean. These German cruisers, the most famous of which were the *Karlsruhe*, *Dresden* and *Emden*, raided shore installations and sank Allied merchant ships.

When Japan entered the war on the side of the Allies in 1914, her forces occupied the German naval base of Tsingtao on the Chinese coast. As a result, Admiral von Spee's squadron, which had been based there, was forced to put to sea and travelled the Pacific Ocean in search of Allied merchant shipping and wrought havoc by attacking British and French shore installations. From time to time, von Spee's ships had to put into harbour to take on coal and food and on one occasion bought supplies from a British trader who was unaware there was a war taking place. In November 1914, von Spee's squadron met up with three British cruisers under Admiral Craddock off the coast of Chile and at the Battle of Coronel, the Germans won an impressive victory and sank all three British cruisers. Out for revenge, a large British force set out and caught up with the Germans in the south Atlantic. The Battle of the Falkland Islands was a major British success and only one German ship escaped and von Spee, together with his two sons and 2,000 sailors, drowned. In the Indian Ocean, the German battleship *Königsberg*, threatened British shipping heading for the Suez Canal. Amongst her victims was the *City of Winchester* that was carrying most of the Ceylon tea crop and she also managed to delay the first Australian and New Zealand troops bound for Europe. Spotted from the air, the *Königsberg* was finally cornered and forced to scuttle in the mouth of the River Rufifi in German East Africa. Yet another German raider, the *Karlsruhe*, attacked Allied shipping until she unaccountably blew up and sank taking with her virtually all her crew. The *Dresden* evaded her pursuers by hiding in the inlets along the Chilean coast until she too was tracked down and forced to scuttle off Juan Fernandez Island in the Pacific.

By far the most famous and successful of all the German surface raiders was the *Emden*. Known as the 'Swan of the East', the *Emden* was an impressive cruiser commanded by a skilful and chivalrous captain, Karl von Muller. He asked permission to act independently and raid shipping in the Indian Ocean and von Spee agreed telling him that 'there are great prizes to be won'. In order to disguise his ship, von Muller added a dummy funnel so that, from a distance, it resembled a British warship and then, sailing southward across the Pacific, the *Emden* reached the Indian Ocean and bombarded Madras where it set fire to

50,000 tonnes of petroleum. The raider next entered Penang harbour in the Malay peninsular and there sank a Russian cruiser and a French destroyer. During the next seven weeks, the *Emden* sank a further 19 British merchantmen representing 70,000 tonnes of shipping. British, French, Japanese and Russian ships jointly organized a search for her and in November 1914, the German warship came face to face with the faster and heavier Australian cruiser, HMAS *Sydney*. Driven aground on a reef in the Cook Islands, von Muller surrendered but some of his crew managed to escape and after an incredible adventure made their way to Arabia before finally reaching Germany.

The Battle of Jutland

The Battle of Jutland, known to the Germans as the Battle of Skagerrak, was the only major sea battle of the First World War. Until this time, the British Grand Fleet and German High Seas Fleet had avoided a direct confrontation but this came to an end during the afternoon of 31 May 1916 when a German fleet under Admiral Reinhard Scheer faced a British fleet under Admiral Jellicoe in the North Sea off Jutland.

The German plan was to bait a trap and tempt Admiral Beatty's battlecruiser squadron out of Rosyth in the belief that it was chasing a relatively small German force. Von Hipper, the commander of the German squadron, would then retire with Beatty in hot pursuit and so draw him unwittingly towards the main German fleet that was some 80 kilometres (50 miles) distant over the horizon. Beatty's ships would then be easily overwhelmed. The Germans were unaware that the British, with access to their secret codes, knew of their plan and were planning a trap of their own by using a near identical plan. Von Hipper did not realize that the bulk of the British Grand Fleet had also put to sea at the same time as Beatty and was out of sight but not far distant from his squadron.

The Battle of Jutland was fought in two phases. In the first, the squadrons of Beatty and Hipper confronted each other until the German admiral ordered his ships to turn about and so draw Beatty towards the German High Seas Fleet. During the long-range duel that followed, the Royal Navy lost two battleships, HMS *Indefatigable* and HMS *Queen Mary*. However, with von Hipper in difficulties, Scheer ordered the German High Seas Fleet to steam forward to support him without realizing that

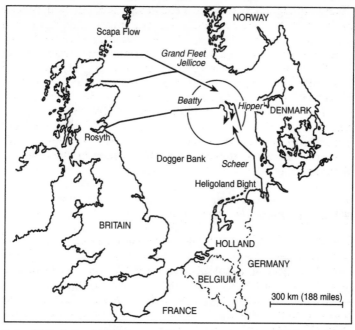

figure 17 the Battle of Jutland

just beyond Beatty's squadron lay Jellicoe with the British Grand Fleet. The second phase of the battle began when the German fleet came face to face with the main British force. With the British fleet approaching in six lines ahead, Jellicoe immediately ordered his ships to turn to port, to the left, to form an extended line side by side since this would allow them to fire broadside after broadside at the leading ships as they came within range. Outlined against the evening sky, they were easy targets and Sheer, fearing that his fleet might be totally destroyed, ordered his fleet to retire. Battle was later resumed with the ships of both sides milling around firing at each other. Meanwhile, Jellicoe took the opportunity to cut off Scheer's line of retreat by placing some of his ships between the German fleet and their home ports. With dense smoke and the coming of nightfall making visibility increasingly difficult, Jellicoe was forced to alter course to avoid a mass torpedo attack. Once it was dark, Scheer's fleet broke through the British line and disappeared into the night and the next morning Jellicoe's warships searched the sea for remnants of the German fleet but found nothing. Scheer's High Seas Fleet was safely back in port.

Comparative British and German losses at Jutland

	British losses	German losses
Battleships	0	1
Battlecruisers	3	0
Cruisers	3	5
Destroyers	8	5
Tonnage	115,025	61,180
Lives	6,097	2,545

And so who won? After the battle both sides claimed victory. Without doubt, the Royal Navy's losses were considerably greater than those of the German fleet. From Jellicoe's viewpoint, a major tragedy was the loss of three battlecruisers, *Indefatigable*, *Queen Mary and Invincible*, each of which received direct hits that resulted in massive explosions and the ships sank in 30 seconds and with great loss of life. In the case of the *Invincible*, there were only six survivors and when the cruiser *Black Prince* sank, there were none. This provided proof of the inadequacy of the armour on such ships and consequently their inability to withstand direct hits. The German battleships were built with watertight compartments and it was possible to flood the magazines in the event of an imminent threat from exploding shells. The battle also provided evidence of the superiority of German shells and the quality of their gunnery. Later, some blamed Jellicoe for being too cautious in not giving chase to the German fleet when it fled but this is not entirely fair since the British admiral faced the possibility that his ships were being drawn into a trap set by German submarines. In addition, throughout the battle Jellicoe suffered from a lack of up-to-date intelligence so that he had no idea what was going on and with none of his ships reporting directly to him, crucial information that might have helped to locate the enemy failed to reach him. Statistically, the Germans might appear to have a case for claiming the Battle of Jutland as a victory but in reality the real honours went to the Royal Navy. The German fleet had fled and been driven from the high seas. A disgruntled British naval captain lamented, 'We had them stone cold and we let them go.' The neutral press more fairly commented, 'The German fleet has assaulted its jailer, but is still in jail.' Afterwards, British command of the seas was never again seriously challenged since the German fleet never again risked a major confrontation and spent the rest of the war penned up in its ports. However, below the waves it was to be a different matter since the Germans had no alternative but to intensify their submarine campaign against the Allies.

The heroism of 16-year-old John Cornwell

John Travers Cornwell, or Jack as he was usually called, was born at Leyton in Essex in 1900. After briefly working as a delivery boy, at the age of 15 he joined the Royal Navy. As a Boy 2nd Class, he earned two and a half pence a week and all found (food and clothing provided) but after gunnery training he was promoted to Boy 1st Class and his pay doubled. At the time of the Battle of Jutland, he was serving on HMS *Chester* and during the course of the battle, his ship was in the thick of the fighting and received several direct hits. John Cornwell was in the forward gun turret when a shell exploded, killed most of the gun crew and left him badly wounded. In spite of his wounds, surrounded by the dead and dying, he stayed at his post waiting for any commands that might come. Once back in harbour, he was rushed to a Grimsby hospital but died the next day. After an impressive funeral, he was buried in Manor Park Cemetery and later his mother received his posthumous Victoria Cross on his behalf. Afterwards, the Boy Scout movement instituted the Cornwell Badge as the highest award that can be made to a Boy Scout for courage and devotion. Sadly two years later, his brother, Arthur Cornwell, was killed in action in France.

An unhappy postscript to the Battle of Jutland was that on 6 June, barely a week after the battle, Lord Kitchener and his staff were drowned when the cruiser HMS *Hampshire* struck a mine and sank off the Orkney Islands. Some mystery surrounds the sinking of the *Hampshire*, which was taking Kitchener on a secret mission to Russia. Was it a chance occurrence or was it, as some maintain, the result of German espionage?

Naval blockades

The aim of a blockade is to cripple the enemy's economy and starve the people into submission by denying them supplies of raw materials and foodstuffs. For the Allies, it was relatively easy for them to enforce a blockade of Germany and Austria-Hungary. With hostile powers on three sides – Russia to the east, Italy to the south and France to the west – it was left to the Allies to complete the blockade by closing the North Sea and Mediterranean Sea to German shipping. In order to accomplish this, a series of minefields was placed across the entrance to the Straits of Dover, off the coast of German-occupied Belgium and in the North Sea between the Scottish coast and Norway. A decision to intercept and board neutral shipping in search of goods likely to assist the German war effort led to difficulties and in this respect, the British government had to be particularly cautious with complaints from the United States. Nevertheless, the Allied blockade was successful and as the war progressed so the German people began to experience acute shortages which led to widespread food riots. The security of the English Channel was the responsibility of the Dover Patrol, a squadron of destroyers and minesweepers. Being an island people, the Germans were quick to recognize the vulnerability of Britain to a submarine-enforced blockade.

The German U-boat campaign against Britain

Even before the twentieth century there had been numerous attempts to build a craft capable of operating under water, but most ended in disaster and some proved fatal to their crews. Submarines submerge by flooding their ballast tanks and surface by blowing out the water with compressed air. On top is a conning tower with watertight hatches and when submerged, a periscope is used to survey the sea. The most important attributes of a submarine are that it can submerge quickly when spotted by the enemy and that, within limits, it can withstand water pressure and the threat posed by exploding depth charges. The first submarines in operational service were British K-boats but driven by steam engines, the fires of which had to be extinguished before it could dive, they were far from reliable and once the war started, more K-boats were lost due to mechanical failure than enemy action. Driven by diesel engines, German U-boats were far better designed. Although both K-boats and U-boats carried torpedoes, their main armament was a single deck gun. This meant that submarines had to come to the surface in order to engage the enemy. The problem with the torpedo was that is was unreliable and likely to go off course or fail to explode when it hit its intended target. However, when it did explode, it was extremely effective. In the Royal Navy, K-boats soon gave way to E Class submarines and these were to be mainly responsible for the contribution made by British submarines to the war at sea. These had the appearance of a more modern submarine and were powered by turbines when on the surface and an electric motor when submerged. Like all submarines, they travelled more quickly on the surface than when under water. Some submarines were used as minelayers and towards the end of the war experiments were made to discover if they could carry seaplanes.

Although at the start of the war the German navy possessed only 30 U-boats (*Untersee* boats), they had an abundance of targets to attack. The first submarine action occurred in August 1914 when HMS *Birmingham* sank the U15 but this was avenged the following month when the U21 sank the British warship, HMS *Pathfinder*. October saw the start of a new phase in the German submarine campaign when the U17 sank a British merchant ship, the *Glitra*. At this stage of the war, German U-boats surfaced in order to attack merchant ships and the crews were allowed to take to the lifeboats before their ships were sunk but this conduct did not last long. The Germans next began a period of unrestricted submarine action by declaring the seas around Britain to be a 'war zone' and warning that ships entering those waters were liable to be sunk without warning. On 7 May 1915, the Cunard liner, *Lusitania*, was torpedoed off the southern coast of Ireland.

The sinking of the *Lusitania*

On 1 May 1915, the British liner *Lusitania* sailed from New York bound for Liverpool. The Cunard liner, the largest and fastest on the transatlantic service, was carrying 1,906 passengers and crew. In New York, the German embassy had published a warning that the ship was likely to be attacked. Ironically, in some American newspapers the notice appeared next to an advertisement promoting the voyage and giving details of the liner's sailing times. Early on the afternoon of the 7 May, the liner was torpedoed by the German submarine U20 off the coast of southern Ireland. The *Lusitania* sank in 18 minutes taking with her 1,098 passengers and crew of which 128 were Americans. In the United States there was an outcry and a wave of anti-German feeling swept the country but in Germany, the press described the sinking as an 'outstanding success' and a medal was struck to commemorate the U-boat's achievement. Since that time there has been a great deal of controversy surrounding the sinking of the *Lusitania*. Why did the ship sink so quickly? Why was there such great loss of life when the ship was in sight of land? The liner's captain, William Turner, claimed that two torpedoes struck the *Lusitania* but Walter Schweiger, captain of the U20 denied this and said that the second explosion was caused by the detonation of the ship's cargo. Was it possible that the liner was secretly carrying a cargo of armaments and explosives? Whatever the truth, the sinking of the *Lusitania* had the effect of making the American people more supportive of the Allied cause.

The U-boat campaign intensifies

During 1915, German U-boats sank a total of 1,328,985 tonnes of Allied shipping and the monthly total never fell below 300,000 tonnes. Although the Kaiser was uncertain about it and the Chancellor, Bethmann-Hollweg, very much against it, early in 1917, the Germans started a second and far more vigorous period of unrestricted submarine warfare. The German High Command, particularly Ludendorff, was aware that whilst the German armies were engaged in a life and death struggle on the Western Front, large amounts of essential war materials were being carried to Britain on neutral ships. In his view this had to be stopped even if it meant sinking ships bound to British ports from neutral countries and even if it risked bringing the United States into the war, as Americans were still angry at the sinking of the *Lusitania*. Now with 111 U-boats at their disposal, the Germans had even greater success against British shipping. During February 1917, 548,671 tonnes were sunk and in April this rose to a massive 894,147 tonnes with one in every four British merchant ships that left port failing to return. The situation became so serious that it became a real threat to the chances of an Allied victory and with some people doubting Britain's ability to remain in the war, something had to be done.

Allied countermeasures

The entry of the United States into the war changed the situation significantly but even before that, steps had to be taken to deal with the German U-boat menace. David Lloyd George, the British Prime Minister, favoured the introduction of the convoy system. This system would allow merchant ships to group together to sail across the Atlantic protected by a warship escort. Admiral Jellicoe and other high-ranking officers at the Admiralty opposed the idea and argued that a slow-moving convoy would present a bigger target and that German U-boat commanders would have a field day. They also contended that in order to provide escorts, the Grand Fleet would have to give up most of its light cruisers and destroyers and that this would not be in the nation's best interests but in spite of Jellicoe's protests, the convoy system was introduced. Each convoy would consist of some 40 merchant ships surrounded by fast-moving destroyers equipped with depth charges. New tactics and more advanced technology also came into use. Convoys would be protected by both British and American destroyers in home waters with aircraft being used to provide additional cover. Other important developments included the introduction of the hydrophone that made it possible to detect noise under the water and the use of Q-ships. On the face of it, a Q-ship looked like an unarmed merchantman but when it was approached by a U-boat, a range of concealed guns were revealed, capable of blowing its would-be attacker out of the water. The use of Q-ships proved to be a mixed blessing and brought only limited success since U-boat commanders reacted by remaining submerged and invariably used torpedoes to sink their victims without any warning. On the other hand, the introduction of the convoy system was an immediate success. With U-boat commanders no longer able to prey on single defenceless merchant vessels, British losses fell dramatically. By April 1918, the total number of Allied ships launched exceeded the number lost at sea. As Karl Donetz, a U-boat commander said, 'A lone U-boat will sink one or two ships ... but that is a poor percentage of the whole. The convoy would steam on and reach Britain, bringing a rich cargo of foodstuffs and raw materials safely to port.' The German U-boat menace was as good as beaten.

The tragedy of the troopship *Mendi*

During the course of the war, black South Africans were asked to volunteer to serve in the Native Labour Corps on the Western Front. Their function was to dig trenches, build roads and perform other manual tasks but not to engage the enemy in combat. In January 1917, the troopship *Mendi* sailed from Cape Town with 802 members of the South African Labour Corps (SANLC) on board. After calling at Plymouth, the ship set sail for Le Havre and some 18 kilometres (11 miles) off St. Catherine's Point on the Isle of Wight it was in collision in thick fog with the SS *Darro*. As the sea poured into the breach made in the *Mendi*, the ship took only 25 minutes to sink and of the 802 black soldiers on board, 607 were drowned together with

31 of the ship's officers and crew. There is a legend that since there was little chance of many of the men making it to safety, one of their leaders, the Reverend Isaac Wauchope, called them together and said, 'Be quiet and calm, my countrymen, for what is taking place is exactly what you came to do. You are going to die … Raise your war cries brothers, for though they made us leave our assegais in the kraal, our voices are left in our bodies.' The men then removed their boots and sang and danced their death dance on the slanting deck of the sinking ship.

The Zeebrugge raid

Admiral Sir Roger Keyes, the officer in charge of naval operations in the English Channel, planned another measure likely to reduce the U-boat menace. April 1918 witnessed one of the most daring naval actions of the whole war when Keyes led a naval task force to the Belgian port of Zeebrugge with the intention of blockading the Bruges Canal and so reducing the flow of U-boats into the North Sea. His force included the cruiser, HMS *Vindictive*, two passenger ferries carrying additional marines, and three old warships, the *Thetis*, *Intrepid* and *Iphegenia* which had previously been filled with concrete. At Zeebrugge, the marines first went ashore to take possession of the mole and engage the German defences. Then Keyes manoeuvred the three concrete-filled ships into the entrance to the channel, placed them sideways on and then scuttled them. Whilst this was going on, a British submarine managed to edge its way under a viaduct connecting the mole with the mainland and once the crew had abandoned the submarine, it was exploded and the viaduct destroyed and as soon as the marines were on board, the *Vindictive* withdrew under the cover of a smoke screen. The deed ensured that the German troops defending the mole could not be reinforced. In truth, the raid had little effect on the movement of U-boats in and out of Zeebrugge but in Britain the epic action boosted the morale of the people, particularly since it had taken place on St. George's Day. Winston Churchill later referred to the raid as 'an episode unsurpassed in the history of the Royal Navy'. An interesting postscript to the raid was that Keyes recommended the award of eight Victoria Crosses to some of the heroes involved but his recommendation was turned down on the grounds that 'it was too many and risked lowering the standard of the award'. Even so, in the end Keyes had his way and the eight men received their medals.

11

Spads, Fokkers and Camels – the war in the air

This chapter will cover:
- the early development of airships and aeroplanes
- the role of aircraft in the war
- the struggle to achieve aerial supremacy
- the achievements of the 'aces'.

'Thrice cursed War
Which bids that I
Such death should pour
Down from the sky.'

(*Nox Mortis*, Paul Bewsher 1894–1966 who served in the
Royal Naval Air Service)

Airships and aeroplanes – the beginning

Ever since 1783 when the Montgolfier brothers first experimented with hot-air balloons, pioneers tried to make balloon travel a viable proposition. The problem was that balloons were at the mercy of the wind and weather and before any real progress could be made, a means had to be discovered to propel, steer and make balloons capable of carrying passengers and cargo. In 1900, the German, Count Ferdinand von Zeppelin, used a petrol engine to propel a navigable or dirigible balloon. Cigar-shaped, the structure was made of aluminium covered with cotton cloth whilst inside were a number of separate balloon units each filled with hydrogen. The Germans had succeeded in making the first of a fleet of airships or Zeppelins, as they were known, and these were used to provide the first passenger air service. In 1903, at Kitty Hawk, North Carolina, the American aviators Orville and Wilbur Wright made the first flight in a heavier-than-air machine that lasted 59 seconds as the aircraft travelled some 260 metres (853 feet). Two years later, the brothers designed *Flier III*, which was a more practical aircraft capable of banking and turning and could reach a speed of 56 kilometres (35 miles) an hour. They brought their famous *Flier III* to Europe and flew it in public. In Britain, it was an American, the self-styled 'Colonel' S. F. Cody who first completed a powered flight. More spectacular was the flight of the Frenchman Louis Blériot across the English Channel in 1909 that attracted much public attention and first focused the minds of the military on the potential of aircraft as a weapon of war. In a remarkably short time, an assortment of monoplanes, biplanes, triplanes and even seaplanes were designed and made available. The threat of a European war accelerated the development of both airships and aircraft for military purposes.

Early days – the Royal Flying Corps

Before having an identity of its own, the Royal Flying Corps (RFC) was originally an army unit and existed firstly as a Balloon Section and then as the Air Battalion of the Royal Engineers whilst the Royal Navy had its own branch, the Royal Naval Air Service. The pilots and observers needed to serve in the new units were mainly recruited from upper-class families who had access to an aircraft and regarded flying as a hobby; the engineers came from the ranks of skilled tradesmen who would have previously been engaged in vehicle maintenance or such trades as map-making and photography. The majority of British aircraft was made by either the Royal Aircraft Factory at Farnborough or by privately-owned companies such as Sopwith Aviation and De Havilland. In 1914, at the start of the war, four squadrons of aircraft with a total strength of 63 aeroplanes flown and maintained by 860 men, crossed to France to serve with the BEF. Most of their aircraft were two seaters with a maximum speed of just under 100 kilometres (62 miles) an hour that could fly at a height of 1,000 metres (3,281 feet). At that time, the French had 138 operational aircraft and the Germans 230. Aerodromes were no more than fields with maintenance buildings and living accommodation close by.

The role of aircraft

To start with, men were placed in baskets suspended beneath balloons to keep a watch on the enemy's activities. Winched up to a suitable height, the unfortunate men were clearly visible to the enemy and became the targets of both ground troops and aircraft. In the event of their situation becoming too hazardous, they were issued with parachutes to allow them to make a hasty, if perilous, descent. It was originally thought that aircraft should only be used for observation and reconnaissance and no one imagined that they would become involved in aerial combat. During the opening phase of the war, aircraft quickly demonstrated their tactical value when in 1914 they warned the British and French of the German advance on Mons and it was French aircraft that first reported the change in direction taken by the German army and allowed the decisive Allied counterattack on the Marne. In a dispatch, Sir John French noted that aircraft had 'been of incalculable value in the conduct of operations'. Once the situation on the Western Front reached stalemate, aircraft were increasingly used for spotting targets, directing artillery fire and keeping a lookout for troop concentrations or any general movement that might indicate that preparations were being made for an offensive. At first, communications between aircraft and command posts on the ground were maintained either by dropping weighted messages or the use of signalling lamps but once introduced, the use of wireless proved much more effective. The system used for reporting ground positions was known as the 'clock code' by which the area around the target was divided into imaginary circles and each circle allocated a letter to show its distance from the centre. On all operations, pilots and observers were armed with rifles and revolvers.

Since photographs could be closely examined on the ground, aerial photography was essential for gathering accurate military intelligence. Aircraft flew over the enemy lines photographing their trench positions and troop concentrations but it was far from an easy task since the cameras were large, difficult to handle and attached to the outside of the aircraft. In spite of the fact that aircraft flying on such missions came under intense enemy fire from the ground, aerial photography made it possible to produce much-needed detailed trench maps.

From the spring of 1915, aircraft became increasingly involved in strafing enemy positions with machine-gun fire and dropping bombs on supply lines, ammunition dumps and road and railway communications. They were often criticized by the infantry on the ground since their activities were liable to stir up trouble along sections of the line that had previously been quiet. Soldiers also resented the fact that, their missions completed, fliers were able to return to their bases well behind the lines and spend their evenings in the comfort of the officers' mess or a local *estaminet*. The soldiers also disliked the apparent camaraderie shown by fliers on both sides who sometimes seemed more inclined to wave than shoot each other down. There were occasions when pilots that had been shot down were collected and allowed to join in their enemy's celebrations. Infantryman thought that airmen were not involved in the real war and there were times when this bad feeling spilled over into brawls.

Skirmishing and dogfights

To start with there was little fighting between the fliers on both sides but this situation did not last long and soon the skies over the Western Front became the scene of skirmishing between individual aircraft and mass dogfights between whole squadrons. Success in the sky depended on the quality of the aircraft and the individual skill of the pilots. In an aircraft, the crew, usually the pilot and an observer who acted as a gunner, sat in open cockpits and were fully exposed to the elements. Quite incredibly, aircrews were not equipped with parachutes since they were thought to be un-British and liable to undermine the pilot's determination to stay with his aircraft. In most aeroplanes, the fuel tank was situated close to the engine and sometimes directly under the pilot's seat so that with no means of escape from a blazing aircraft, men were liable to become human torches and suffer horrendous burns. Armed only with light weapons – revolvers and rifles – the best fliers could do was take pot shots at other aircraft. Soon British aeroplanes were equipped with Lewis guns fixed to the side of the aircraft or in the case of a biplane, on the upper wing which meant that firing directly ahead involved a risk of shooting off the aircraft's propeller. Some advance was made when propeller blades were fitted with steel blades intended to deflect bullets but the real breakthrough came when a Dutchman, Anthony Fokker, invented an interrupter gear that he supplied to the Germans. This ingenious innovation momentarily prevented the plane's machine gun from firing when the propeller blade passed in front of it.

Solo scouting missions soon gave way to more offensive operations. In order to make the planes less vulnerable to sudden attack, the leader flew at the front of a V-shaped formation and with the remaining aircraft behind in close proximity. When engaging the enemy, the squadron would break up and, left to his own devices, each pilot engaged in individual combat. In dogfights, tactics and manoeuvrability were all important whilst additional height allowed an aircraft to gain extra speed as it swooped on an unsuspecting enemy. The use of cloud cover was also important as was the advantage of having the sun at one's back and Allied pilots were warned, 'Beware of the Hun in the sun'. Aircraft were lightweight and this meant that when in difficulty it was possible for a pilot to land his plane in a field and take off again once it was safe. Since German pilots were equipped with parachutes and they seldom flew beyond the limits of their own front line, their survival rate was considerably higher than that of the British. There were stages in the war when the casualty rates were such that the life expectancy of inexperienced RFC pilots was only a few weeks.

During 1916, the RFC lost an average of two pilots every day and the situation worsened to the extent that during the following year, 50 aircraft were lost weekly. Towards the end of the war German tactics changed when they took to flying in mass formation. Impressive to look at but not over successful, the most famous group was nicknamed 'Richthofen's Flying Circus'.

The struggle for air supremacy

Although pilots became increasingly skilled, their ability in aerial combat counted for little if they did not possess the fastest, most manoeuvrable and best armed aircraft and so as the war progressed, the advantage swung from one side to the other. At the start of the war, both the British DH2 and the French Spad proved adequate but the advantage passed to the Germans when they introduced the Fokker Eindecker equipped with interrupter gear. So superior was the 'Fokker Scourge' in combat that Allied fliers came to regard themselves as nothing more than 'Fokker Fodder' but this changed in 1916 when the French developed the Nieuport XVII and the British the DH4. Before the end of the year the Germans were again able to claim the upper hand with the introduction of the twin-gunned Albatros. During the following months this aircraft wrought havoc and in April 1917, 'Bloody April' as it came to be known, the fortunes of the RFC and French Air Service reached their lowest ebb. Fortunately, the arrival of better designed and armed aircraft including the Sopwith Camel once again turned the tables in favour of the Allies. The Sopwith Camel, so called because of a hump on its fuselage, could out-manoeuvre German fighters in a dogfight and by the end of the war had accounted for 1,294 enemy aircraft. The Germans did produce what might have proved to be an even more superior aircraft, the Fokker CDII, but thankfully, for the Allies, it failed to get it into production in time.

The 'Aces'

Faster and more sophisticated aircraft created a new breed of airmen who developed their own distinctive tactics, the extremely skilled and equally ruthless 'aces'. Irrespective of their skills, the status of an 'ace' depended on the number of enemy aircraft he managed to shoot down and this he indicated with markings on the side of his aircraft's fuselage. Each country had its legendary 'aces' who became contemporary folk heroes. The most famous were the German, Manfred von Richthofen, the Frenchman, Georges Guynemer, and the Briton, Albert Ball.

A regular soldier who had once served in the trenches, Manfred von Richtofen learned his flying skills from another pilot with whom he had earlier flown as an observer. Leader of the famous Richthofen Squadron, he flew in an Albatros and, as if to flaunt his ability, he painted the fuselage bright red. Nicknamed the 'Red Baron' by the British and the 'Red Devil' by the French, during his wartime career, he shot down 80 Allied aircraft. He was finally shot down as he flew over the trenches in pursuit of a British aircraft. A great deal of controversy exists and many books have been written regarding who was responsible for shooting down his aircraft. Credit first went to a Canadian pilot, Captain Arthur Brown, but this was contested by Australians who claim that one of their gunners shot down Richthofen's plane with a single bullet fired from a machine gun in the trenches. A British pilot flew over the German aerodrome and dropped a note informing the Germans of the Red Baron's death. He was first buried in France with full military honours but after the war his body was exhumed and reburied in the family cemetery at Wiesbaden. On Richthofen's death, leadership of his squadron passed to Hermann Goering who later was to become a leading Nazi and commanded the German airforce, the *Luftwaffe*, during the Second World War.

Originally declared physically unfit and rejected for military services, Georges Guynemer eventually succeeded in joining the French Air Service as a mechanic before qualifying as a pilot. Three months later, he destroyed his first German aircraft but then was himself shot down. During the Battle of Verdun, he had a further eight victories and was fortunate to survive a crash landing. By mid-1917, his total score had reached 30 and included four enemy aircraft shot down in one day but by this time his poor health had further deteriorated and his family and superiors urged him to retire. He refused and five days after claiming his fifty-fourth victim, he was shot down and his body never found. The French pilot with the greatest number of victories, his countrymen considered him the 'Ace of Aces'.

The best-known British fighter pilot of the war, Albert Ball, came from Lenton in Nottinghamshire and served with the Sherwood Foresters before transferring to the Royal Flying Corps. Unlike Richthofen and Guynemer, Albert Ball was an individualist who preferred to fly alone. Consequently 60 Squadron allowed him free range and he was known to attack the enemy regardless of their number and the odds stacked against him. On one occasion, he took on six enemy aircraft single-handed and it was said that at times he appeared to be waging a private war against the German air force. His favourite ploy was to dive steeply, position himself behind and just below his enemy and rake the underside of his opponent's aircraft with machine-gun fire. Something of a loner, he was a quiet man whose favourite form of relaxation was playing the violin. During his career, he destroyed 11 enemy aircraft and forced numerous others to land. Ball was awarded the DSO and two bars, the Military Cross and the Victoria Cross. Still aged only 21, he was killed in action in France in May 1917.

Bombers and bombing raids

Neither side felt bound by the Hague Convention of 1899 that prohibited 'the dropping of projectiles and explosives from flying machines'. At the start of the war the Germans had a force of 30 airships or Zeppelins. Between 150 and 250 metres (492 and 820 feet) long and containing up to 56,000 cubic metres (two million cubic feet) of highly-flammable hydrogen, they might appear to have been easy targets but they were reasonably safe from attack from the ground or by aircraft because of the height at which they flew. In September 1914, the British made the first move when their aircraft attacked Zeppelin sheds at Dusseldorf and Cologne and followed this up with more widespread raids in Germany. To begin with, bombs were dropped manually over the side of the aircraft and even when bomb-aiming apparatus was introduced, it was extremely primitive and inaccurate. The Germans reacted to the British raids by using Zeppelins as terror weapons to attack purely civilian targets. The first raid on Britain came in May 1915 when Zeppelins bombed London and succeeded in killing five people and starting some fires. Afterwards there were more substantial raids on the Midlands, East Coast and again on London during which 556 civilians were killed. In spite of the public outcry, there was little that could be done to prevent them since Zeppelins carried out their raids on moonlit nights and at that stage of the war, the British had no night fighters. To those who flew Zeppelins, bad weather was more of a danger than enemy action although the British did have some successes.

Sub-Lieutenant Reginald Warneford was the first to shoot down a Zeppelin when he caught it flying at lower altitude over Belgium and managed to bomb it from above. As the war progressed, a defensive system was gradually put in place around London that included anti-aircraft guns, searchlights and barrage balloons. Then in 1917, 11 Zeppelins were caught in a violent storm and all were lost. Afterwards the Germans began to phase them out and replace them with bomber aircraft, the most famous of which was the Gotha. During the last year of the war these aircraft carried out numerous raids against London and south-east England and were responsible for nearly 3,000 casualties. A new British bomber, the Handley Page, with a range of over 2,000 kilometres (1,243 miles) brought Berlin within striking distance but the war came to an end before it was operational.

During the course of the war, the importance of aircraft became increasingly evident. The tactical use of air power and its ability to influence the outcome of a battle indicated that aeroplanes had come of age. In 1918, the Royal Flying Corps and the Royal Naval Air Service were combined to become a separate branch of the armed services, the Royal Air Force (RAF).

12

'keep the home fires burning' – the home front

This chapter will cover:
- the British reaction to the war
- the problems that faced the British government
- the Easter Rebellion in Ireland
- the issue of conscription
- the extent to which the war affected the everyday lives of the British people.

'Keep the home fires burning
  While your hearts are yearning
Though your lads are far away,
  They dream of home.'

(A popular song, *Keep the Home Fires Burning*,
written by Ivor Novello, 1893–1951)

Britain at the start of the war

In 1914, at the outbreak of war, Britain had a Liberal government led by Herbert Asquith. Other leading members of the government included David Lloyd George, Chancellor of the Exchequer, Sir Edward Grey, Foreign Secretary, and Winston Churchill, First Lord of the Admiralty whilst Lord Kitchener was appointed Secretary for War. The declaration of war led to a wave of anti-German feeling that sometimes turned to mindless hysteria. People with German-sounding names had their windows smashed and their businesses ransacked, lecturers of German or Austrian origin were abused by their students even if they had long been naturalized British citizens. Many, even though they were old and infirm, were interned and some were even driven to suicide. The writer D. H. Lawrence was insulted because his wife was a member of the Richthofen family; Prince Louis of Battenberg, forced to resign from the Royal Navy because of his German connections, changed his family name to Mountbatten. The Royal Automobile Club (RAC) banned members of German or Austrian origin and it was even considered unpatriotic to own a dachshund dog. In his magazine *John Bull*, Horatio Bottomley advised his readers, 'if one day in a restaurant you are being served by a German waiter, you will throw your soup in his foul face; if you find yourself sitting next to a German clerk, you will spill the inkpot over his foul head'. At the same time the country was affected by spy mania and much of this was caused by the appearance of Erskine Childers's espionage novel, *The Riddle of the Sands* (1900), and the irresponsible writing of William Le Queux.

To cope with the situation, the government passed the Defence of the Realm Act (DORA) which allowed the use of an extensive range of emergency powers. For serious crimes, civilians became liable to trial by courts martial and for lesser crimes, by summary trial and punishment. Whilst steps were taken to protect railways and ports from acts of espionage, the censorship of all outward-bound overseas mail was introduced to prevent people communicating with the enemy. Censorship of the press was also introduced and action taken to control the sale of alcohol. Measures were also taken to prevent the spread of false rumours and powers were granted to the government to requisition factories and workshops and turn them to wartime production.

Early problems

The appointment of Lord Kitchener as Secretary for War created problems. The choice of the hero of the Battle of Omdurman and the Boer War was intended to provide a boost to the morale of the British people and to his credit, he recognized that it would be a prolonged war and his famous 'Your country needs you' poster inspired thousands to volunteer to serve in the forces. An aloof man who resented criticism, he proved difficult to work with since he held the view that he should be allowed to run the war by himself without interference or a need to consult his Cabinet colleagues. He refused to delegate responsibility, treated his subordinates with contempt and was even at loggerheads with Lloyd George. As far as the nation was concerned, his untimely death in 1916 was regarded as a tragedy but as one observer commented, 'it was not so much regretted in government and by his friends, not at all, for he never had any.' Margot Asquith, the Prime Minister's wife said of Kitchener's death, 'if he was not a great man, he was a great poster'.

In 1915, Field Marshal Sir John French let it be known in *The Times* newspaper that the main reason for his lack of success on the Western Front was an acute shortage of shells. This disclosure led to public disquiet, open criticism of the government, a crisis of confidence and the end of the Liberal government. In its place, Asquith set up a coalition government with a Cabinet consisting of Liberals, Conservatives and the leader of the Labour Party, Arthur Henderson. David Lloyd George was appointed Minister of Munitions. The mercurial Welshman took control of all munitions factories and, against considerable trade-union opposition, used his persuasive skills to do away with a range of restrictive practices and encouraged the employment of women. More inclined to use businessmen than civil servants to run the factories, Lloyd George's management of the munitions industry was impressive. Earlier, Kitchener had commented that four machine guns per battalion would be sufficient and anything more a luxury. Lloyd George, determined to exceed this, famously said, 'Take Kitchener's figure. Square it.

Multiply by two. Then double it again for luck.' A. J. P. Taylor (1954) summed up his achievement, 'The army began the war with 1,330 machine guns. During the war 240,506 were manufactured – thanks to Lloyd George.' Lloyd George was also responsible for a range of measures taken to combat absenteeism due to drunkenness by reducing licensing hours, diluting the strength of beer and imposing heavier taxes on alcoholic drinks. King George gave his campaign a boost by banning the consumption of alcohol in the royal household but the Houses of Parliament declined to follow the sovereign's example.

Women go to war

British trade-union leaders feared that the permanent employment of women in the workplace might bring about the dilution of industry and lead to unemployment when servicemen were demobilized at the end of the war. Some also feared the consequences of the additional independence women might gain by having their own pay packets. Women were not just employed in the manufacture of munitions but in many other positions vacated by men serving at the front. In the munitions factories, girls worked 12-hour shifts, seven days a week for a wage of £2.20, just half that paid to men doing the same work but nearly three times that paid to soldiers serving in the trenches. The task of filling shell cases with explosives was not without its dangers and the powder turned the faces of the girls bright yellow and earned them the nickname 'canary girls'. There were also major disasters when an explosion at a munitions works at Chilwell in Nottinghamshire killed 250 and another at Silvertown in London's East End claimed over 300 lives. The idea of them being a 'gentle sex' was abandoned as women worked in a range of heavy industries, delivered coal, collected refuse, operated buses and trains and were employed in agriculture as Land Girls. Many volunteered to become nurses and towards the end of the war they were allowed to enrol in the services as uniformed auxiliaries. Altogether 92,000 joined the Women's Army Auxiliary Corps (WAAC), the Women's Royal Naval Service (WRNS) and the Women's Royal Air Force (WRAF). With many young girls living away from home in hostels, the employment of women on such a large scale created social problems and there was concern about their moral welfare. The work of such organizations as the Women's Patrol and the Women's League of Honour failed to prevent a

30 per cent increase in the illegitimacy rate of children born during the war years. Living away from their homes and their parents allowed girls a greater freedom that brought with it changes in their attitudes and outlook. The wearing of cosmetics and smoking became widespread as did drinking in public houses whilst dress-wise, the wearing of long skirts and camisoles gave way to short skirts and brassieres. Some young women also used language that would have shocked their parents and grandparents. It is estimated that in the final year of the war over 1.3 million women were in employment with over half of them doing jobs previously done by men.

The Easter Rebellion of 1916

In 1914, it seemed that the long-standing Irish demand for home rule was about to be granted but when the war started Asquith's government declared that the issue would have to be suspended until the conflict was over. In the event, both those who favoured home rule, the Irish Nationalists, and those against, the Unionists, declared their support for Britain in her war 'for the freedom of small nations' and some 80,000 Irishmen volunteered to serve in the British army. Many of them were Irish Nationalists only too pleased to fight for the independence of largely Catholic Belgium but home in Ireland there were still those who resented the British government's decision to suspend the granting of home rule.

Amongst a group known as the Irish Volunteers were men who regarded the coming of war as an opportunity to force the hand of the British government since they believed that 'England's difficulty was Ireland's opportunity'. The leaders of these men, Patrick Pearse, Sean McDermott and James Connolly, set about planning a rebellion against continued British rule. Their cause was helped by the fact that the British government was considering the introduction of conscription and this would have meant that Irishmen would have been forced to serve in the British armed forces. As preparations were made for the rebellion, so the Irish Volunteers paraded openly, collected money to buy weapons from Germany and tried to recruit men for a Citizens' Army. The rebellion was planned to take place on Easter Sunday 1916 when men would take over strategic points in the centre of Dublin and surround the British army barracks in Dublin Castle. The rebel headquarters was to be the General Post Office in Sackville Street, now known as O'Connell Street.

The uprising got off to a bad start when a German gun-running ship was intercepted by the Royal Navy. Even so, events went ahead as planned and on Easter Sunday morning people watched as the rebels ran up the Irish green orange and white tricolour over the post office and Pearse read a proclamation declaring the establishment of an Irish Republic. With none of the promised German assistance forthcoming, the rebels were hopelessly outnumbered and one by one their strongholds were overrun by British troops. From Dublin Bay, salvos (gunfire from ships) from a Royal Navy gunboat reduced the centre of the city to rubble and a mass of flames. On 29 April, the Irish Volunteers surrendered unconditionally.

The rebellion, which cost the lives of 550 people and left over 2,500 wounded, also caused damage to buildings and property at an estimated cost of £3 million. Arrests followed and although 90 people were sentenced to death only 15 were actually executed. One of those put on trial was a former British diplomat who had earlier been awarded a knighthood, Sir Roger Casement. In spite of his Protestant Ulster origins, he sympathized with the aims of the Irish Nationalist movement and had gone as far as to travel to Germany to win support for the rebellion and urge Irish prisoners of war to form a brigade to fight against the British. His mission proved a failure and he returned to Ireland to try and prevent the uprising that he was now convinced was doomed to failure. Soon after he was put ashore from a German submarine in Tralee Bay, Casement was arrested and sent for trial at the Old Bailey in London charged with treason. At his trial, he presented his case well but the appearance of his diaries containing details of his homosexual activities proved decisive. He was found guilty and hanged in Pentonville prison. To this day, the authenticity of Casement's diaries remains disputed and to the Irish, he is considered a patriot and martyr to the cause of their independence.

The bulk of the Irish people had not supported the rebellion and they were angry that their lives had been put at risk and their homes destroyed because of it. However, when it became known that British soldiers had shot some prisoners out of hand, imprisoned many blameless men and that James Connolly, too weak to stand, had been tied to a chair to face his executioners, sympathy for the rebels increased. Because of his American birth and half-Spanish parentage, one of the leaders of the rebellion to survive was Eamonn de Valera who was later to become Prime Minister and then President of an independent Ireland.

The issue of conscription

In September 1914, Herbert Asquith told the House of Commons that 439,000 men had already volunteered for military service. By the end of that month, this had risen to 750,000 and afterwards the monthly average was 125,000. To some extent these figures were a response to Kitchener's poster but other more subtle methods were also used to encourage men to enlist. Even so, as people became aware of the carnage on the Western Front and the horrific nature of trench warfare, the recruiting posters lost their appeal and ceased to have the same effect. With no longer a rush to enlist, the number of volunteers declined and this meant that the government had to give some thought to the idea of conscripting men for the army.

It was the Earl of Derby who first suggested a scheme by which men were invited to voluntarily register for military service on the understanding that married men would only be called up after all single men on the register. The 'Derby Scheme' failed because whilst married men registered in large numbers few bachelors came forward. Early in 1916, the Military Service Act introduced conscription for all bachelors aged between 18 and 41 and four months later this was extended to all men in that age group. The decision to introduce conscription led to uproar in the House of Commons with a number of Liberal Members of Parliament (MPs) voting against and some senior members of the Cabinet threatening to resign. Across the country branches of a Non-Conscription Fellowship, a movement founded by the Labour MP Fenner Brockway and supported by such notables as Bertrand Russell, Lytton Strachey and Virginia Woolf, were set up. Opposition was based on the fear that conscription would 'militarize the nation' and that it impinged on personal freedom. By the end of the war, conscription had been extended to include men up to the age of 50.

Conscientious objectors

The Military Service Act made provision for men who, for reasons of conscience, were opposed to being conscripted for military service to register as conscientious objectors. Such men, whose objection was usually based on either moral or religious grounds, fell into two categories – alternativists and absolutists. Alternativists were prepared to serve providing they would not be involved in the shedding of blood; the absolutists refused to engage in any form of military service or put on uniform. The alternativists were allowed to join a Non-Combatant Corps and many of them served with distinction in the front line as medical orderlies and lost their lives, but dealing with the absolutists proved a far more difficult matter. Ridiculed as 'conchies' or 'won't fight funks', they had to appear before tribunals usually made up of people who had no sympathy with their viewpoint whatsoever. The questioning was intended to trap men into saying that in certain circumstances they would resort to violence – 'What would you do if a criminal assaulted your mother?' 'What would you do if a stranger attempted to rape your wife?' were typical. The Non-Conscription Fellowship and Quakers offered to coach young men awaiting their tribunals in the art of handling such questioning. Considered cowards, very few succeeded in convincing the tribunals of the validity of their reasons and if they persisted with their objection, they were arrested and sent to prison to serve indeterminate sentences with hard labour. Some were even held in solitary confinement and placed on a diet of bread and water. There were instances when men were forcibly put into uniform and sent to army units in France and, now subject to military law, they were liable to be shot if they refused an order. Although there were rumours, there is no evidence that any conscientious objectors were actually executed.

The effects of the war on the everyday lives of the British people

As a result of towns along the East Coast being shelled by German warships and Zeppelins, and Gotha bombers bombing London and other towns and cities, some 1,500 people had been killed and 3,000 injured by enemy action. Even so, for the vast majority of the people, the war presented no immediate threat to their safety.

During the war it became necessary to ration certain foodstuffs. In spite of the success of the German U-boat campaign, there was never any acute shortage of food and rationing was introduced more to avoid queuing and to assure the people that come what may, everyone would get a fair share of the food available. Even so, sugar was rationed in 1917, meat, butter and tea in 1918 and housewives had to adapt in order to feed their families. In rural areas, food was usually quite plentiful but in the towns and cities a flourishing black market provided extra food and scarce luxuries for those who could afford to pay extra for them. Where foods were in short supply, alternatives had to be found. Margarine replaced butter, white bread became a rarity, horsemeat was eaten and new ways of preserving food used. It was discovered that the dried roots of dandelions provided a powder that tasted something like coffee and that rye bread was not so bad after all. Unfortunately, a tragedy occurred when a housewife decided to cook not only the stalks but also the leaves of rhubarb and succeeded in poisoning her family. In addition, families were encouraged to have meatless days, use government recommended 'war recipes' and above all to avoid wastage. Everyone was encouraged to grow as much food as they could in their gardens and allotments. Fuel and clothing were also scarce and an appeal urged people to 'Take the coal off the fire before you go to bed ... The coal you save today, will start the fire tomorrow.'

With so many men in the armed forces, labour was in short supply and this led to a sharp increase in the earnings of both skilled and unskilled workers so that by 1918, some wages had doubled and in certain industries, even trebled. By mid-1915, food prices had risen by 30 per cent with some scarce foodstuffs more than doubling in price. Worse was to come when by late 1916 food prices had increased by 60 per cent compared with the 1914 level. Even so, wages rose more steeply than prices and generally people were better fed than ever before.

It has been estimated that the war cost the British people a staggering £75,077,000,000. This was paid for out of loans received from the United States and by increasing the money raised from taxation. High taxes were also levied on a wide range of luxury goods. In addition, a patriotic appeal was made to people to help the war effort by purchasing War Bonds.

Apart from providing many women with financial independence, their work in munitions factories and other industries meant that many households now enjoyed a very welcome additional income. In spite of the war, some trade-union leaders, usually those with left-wing views who regarded the conflict as a capitalist war, were prepared to take part in industrial action. Although strikes on Clydeside and in South Wales were settled through conciliation, bitterness remained and strikes in the munitions industry were declared crimes punishable in the courts. It was ironic that the areas that showed most union militancy were the very same areas that had produced the greatest numbers of volunteers for military service.

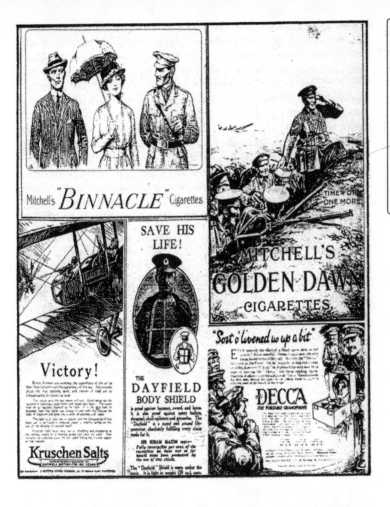

Many adverts showed a complete ignorance of the true nature of soldiering and life at the front. Top (left to right): rival cigarette companies show a young lady obviously preferring the attention of a soldier to that of a civilian; a sergeant treating his men to a final cigarette before going over the top. Bottom (left to right): the heroism of fliers is used to advertise a laxative, Krushen Salts; families were encouraged to buy serving men Dayfield Body Shields which, so the advert claims, will save their lives; an officer 'livens up' his men by playing them music on a Decca gramophone.

As the nation adapted to the needs of wartime production, areas became associated with new manufacturing industries. Whilst munitions factories were widely scattered across the land, the area around the Solent on the South Coast, the Home Counties and Glasgow in Scotland became centres for aircraft production. Whilst Warrington became noted for the production of barbed wire, poison gas was manufactured at Runcorn and the traditional shipbuilding areas in the north-east, north-west, Clydeside and Northern Ireland were called on to produce warships and merchant ships in even greater numbers. As thousands of wounded soldiers returned home to Southampton and other South Coast ports to be treated at Netley and many other hospitals so, for reasons of security, many German prisoners of war were sent to the Isle of Man.

A feature of the war was the speed with which manufacturers adjusted their advertising to embrace the patriotic fervour of the time.

Letters from soldiers serving at the front were often slow to reach home and were censored and often relatives had to make do with the very limited news included on a Field Postcard. News that a relative had been killed in action reached their next of kin by various means. Official notification might take months to arrive and relatives lived in dread of telegrams or letters in buff envelopes that began 'Deeply regret to inform you ...' or 'It is my painful duty to inform you ...'. Before this, such information might have already reached relatives in a letter from one of the soldier's comrades or from an army chaplain who had taken down his last words or attended his burial. It was usual for commanding officers to write personal letters to the wives and mothers of fellow officers who had fallen in battle. A *Weekly Casualty List* was published by the War Office and lists also appeared in local newspapers. Those informed that their relative was 'missing' continued to live in hope but only too often had to finally accept the inevitable. The Germans and the Allies kept each other informed of the details of men who had been taken prisoner.

13

the propaganda war – spies and espionage

This chapter will cover:
- the use of propaganda to influence public attitudes
- anti-German propaganda
- espionage and the activities of German spies
- the unusual cases of Mata Hari and Trebitsch Lincoln.

'For he who lives more lives than one,
more deaths than one must die.'

(*Sonnet to Liberty: Not that I Love Thy Children*,
Oscar Wilde, 1854–1900)

The propaganda war

In the dictionary, propaganda is defined as 'a plan for the spread of opinions and principles especially to effect change and influence behaviour'. In wartime, propaganda can be a powerful weapon and used indiscriminately and without concern for accuracy and honesty, it can reinforce morale and raise false hopes or it can be used to spread false rumours and discredit the enemy. During the war, both the Allies and the Central Powers used propaganda to influence, mislead and outrage public opinion. The British government showed its appreciation of the importance of being able to manipulate public opinion when early in the war, Asquith appointed Charles Masterman to be in charge of propaganda. Propaganda was not just to be used for home consumption, it was intended to influence opinion in neutral countries, particularly the United States and in this, the British had virtually every advantage. Apart from the fact that the two countries shared the same common language, in August 1914, HMS *Telconia* destroyed the transatlantic cable links between Hamburg and New York that ensured that Americans would largely depend on British sources for news about the war.

Anti-German propaganda

Within a month of the outbreak of war, the British popular press carried lurid accounts of German atrocities in Belgium. Obscene stories were told about babies being bayoneted, the mutilation of women and children, the rape of nuns and the boiling of the bodies of British dead in order to use their body fat as grease and tallow. It was claimed that German soldiers had cut off the breasts of a British nurse and left her to die in agony whilst *The Times* carried the story of a Canadian officer who had been crucified to a door with bayonets. The Germans had their own range of atrocity stories that included the gouging out of the eyes of prisoners of war and attempts by the French to infect drinking water with cholera bacilli. It later came to be generally accepted that these stories were untrue yet some very recent research suggests some rumours of German atrocities were not entirely without foundation. At the time, true or not, these

133
the propaganda war –
spies and espionage
13

stories had the desired effect and the British people were convinced that they were involved in a war for civilization against a savage and ruthless enemy, the 'Beastly Hun'. The British were quick to exploit the outrages that they felt sure would offend the American people. Since 128 of the 1,098 passengers drowned were Americans, the sinking of the British liner, *Lusitania*, by a German submarine in May 1915 proved excellent for this purpose. In the United States, the American press published emotive accounts of the suffering and rescue of survivors and expressed its anger at the German action. British propagandists did not let the matter rest and continued to remind Americans that the atrocity was proof of the nature of German barbarism and if further proof was needed it came six months later with the execution of a British nurse, Edith Cavell.

INJURED INNOCENCE.

The German Ogre. "HEAVEN KNOWS THAT I HAD TO DO THIS IN SELF-DEFENCE; IT WAS FORCED UPON ME." (*Aside*) "FEE, FI, FO, FUM!"

A *Punch* cartoon of 1915 depicts the depravity of the 'German Ogre'.

Edith Cavell, who came from Norfolk and was the daughter of a clergyman, became a nurse who went to Belgium to assist in the establishment of a training school for nurses and later became the matron of a hospital in Brussels. At the start of the war, she remained in charge of the hospital and after the city was occupied, she continued to run the hospital and treat both British and German wounded. In August 1915, Edith Cavell was arrested by the Germans and charged with assisting the escape of British soldiers. At her trial, she pleaded guilty and was sentenced to death by shooting. Pleas from the United States, other neutral countries and church leaders that her life be spared were rejected and she was executed on the morning of 12 October 1915. Her famous last words were 'Patriotism is not enough; I must have no hatred or bitterness towards anyone.' One of the German firing squad refused to take part in the deed and was himself later executed.

Following rumours of Belgian atrocities and the loss of civilian lives on the *Lusitania*, the execution of Edith Cavell provided the Allies with further propaganda to stir up anti-German sentiment in the United States. No mention was made of the fact that prior to the execution of the British nurse, the French had already shot three women for their involvement in espionage activities, one of them a nurse.

Spy scares and counterespionage activities

Even before the war, the British people had been alerted to the possibility of German espionage activities by the novels of Erskine Childers and William Le Queux. In Childers' adventure novel, *The Riddle of the Sands* (1900), British yachtsmen sailing amongst the Fresian Islands stumble upon evidence of German plans to invade England and the plot seemed so plausible that two Royal Marine officers on holiday worked their way along the German coast to check for themselves. They were arrested, charged with spying, and imprisoned. Le Queux, whose book *A Secret Service* (1911) was serialized in the *Daily Mail*, claimed that there were already 50,000 German soldiers in Britain masquerading as waiters and tourists. He also warned that a group of British traitors had formed an organization, the 'Hidden Hand', and were ready to work for the Germans and betray their country in the event of a war. Le Queux was one of the favourite authors of the royal family and although his stories were totally fictitious, they caused such a stir that questions were asked in the House of Commons. When war finally broke out in 1914, the country was seething with rumours of German spies and every local newspaper carried details of local spies and their impending arrests. In fact there were no German spies active in Britain at that time but they were soon to arrive.

German spies – the reality

Long before the war, British intelligence services were in place and well prepared to counter any German espionage activities. The eccentric but ruthless Sir Mansfield Cummings ran the under-staffed and under-funded Secret Service and, with one leg amputated, he made his way around his headquarters on a child's scooter. The interrogation expert, Sir Vernon Kell, ran Military Intelligence and was responsible for the introduction of postal censorship. Throughout the war, teams of censors did sterling work inspecting all out-going and in-coming overseas mail at Mount Pleasant in London and were responsible for tracing several important German spies. The master code-breaker Sir Reginald 'Blinker' Hall was head of Naval Intelligence. Described as being 'the one genius the war developed' and that compared with him 'all other secret service men were amateurs', his great scoop was his handling of the Zimmermann telegram that played an important role in bringing the United States into the war (see page 149–50). Special Branch was the responsibility of another formidable interrogator Sir Basil Thomson who had formerly been a diplomat, a tutor to the sons of the King of Siam and a governor of Dartmoor prison. He often seemed more concerned about the activities of subversive groups in Britain than German spies. Some years after the war, he was accused of acts of indecency with prostitutes in Hyde Park, London and although only given a small fine, it left his career in ruins. There is a view that he fell victim of a plot intended to discredit him.

The man in charge of German espionage activities in Britain was the talented Gustav Steinhauer. Before the war he had himself spent a great deal of time in Britain and, posing as a fisherman, had taken pictures of Royal Navy battleships anchored at Scapa Flow. Instead of using German nationals as spies Steinhauer preferred to recruit second-generation Americans whose families were of German origin and English-speaking Scandinavians. German spies, often using stolen or forged passports, had little difficulty getting into Britain since they could travel from the United States, come directly by ferry from neutral Holland, or enter the country by way of Spain, Sweden and Switzerland. A telltale sign of their intentions was that they tended to visit sensitive areas such as ports, shipbuilding yards and military-training areas to report on shipping movements and troop concentrations. Since telegraph was not available to them, their usual methods of getting information back to their operators was by means of coded letters and invisible ink.

Following the outbreak of war, the first German spy to be caught in Britain was the ex-naval officer Karl Hans Lody who, as a former employee of the travel agents, Thomas Cook, spoke English fluently and without the trace of an accent. When he first offered his services to Steinhauer, he was considered unsuitable for espionage work and decided to go it alone on a freelance basis. It is claimed that he was the agent who erroneously reported the arrival of Russian troops in Scotland when, in conversation with a group of soldiers, he failed to understand their accent and thought they said they came from Russia. In fact, they came from Rosshire. Before he was executed by a firing squad in the Tower of London, he wrote a letter of appreciation to the British authorities for 'their kind and considered treatment'. Other German spies who suffered the same fate included the gifted Anton Kupferle who hanged himself in Brixton prison; the German-born naturalized American Georg Breeckow who insisted on a silk blindfold at his execution; and the brilliant Brazilian violinist, Fernando Buschman. Moments before his execution he offered his instrument to a member of the firing squad. The Swedish citizen Ernst Melin chose to spy for the Germans to ease his financial problems and was one of several who insisted on shaking hands with members of the firing squad before his execution. Albert Mayer sang *It's A Long Way To Tipperary* as he went to his execution whilst Irving Reis told the firing squad, 'You are only doing your duty as I have done mine.' Amongst those who spied for the Germans was Courtney de Rysbach. Austrian by birth but a naturalized British subject, he was a music-hall entertainer who sent messages to the Germans by writing between the lines on sheets of music.

Some unusual spies

Mata Hari

The most famous femme fatale in the history of espionage is Mata Hari. Born in 1876 at Leewarden in Holland, the daughter of a milliner, her real name was Gertrude Margaretha Zelle. A precocious girl, she was expelled from school at the age of 14 for seducing her headmaster. As a result of replying to a lonely-hearts advertisement in a local newspaper, she met and married Rudolph Macleod, a Dutch army officer serving in Java, but it proved an unhappy marriage and neglected by her husband, she spent her time learning the arts of oriental dancing. On her return to Holland, she was abandoned by her husband and lived in poverty until she found work as an erotic dancer and part-time prostitute. She took the name Mata Hari, 'Eye of the Dawn', and as her popularity grew, she was engaged to dance at many of the leading nightclubs in Europe where, most spectacularly, she performed the dance of the seven veils and used snakes in part of her act. Being a Dutch citizen, during the war she was able to travel freely in Europe and included amongst her many lovers senior German army officers and French cabinet ministers, including Adolphe-Pierre Messimy, the French Minister for War. It is said that during this time Mata Hari was invited to spy for both the French and Germans. Early in 1917, she was arrested by the French Secret Service and charged with spying for Germany. At her trial, whilst the evidence against her was weak and contradictory, her fate was sealed when her highly-placed lovers refused to testify on her behalf. Found guilty, she was executed at Saint Lazare prison. After the war, the Germans denied that they had ever employed Mata Hari as a spy and it has been suggested that French government spokesmen, or 'spin-doctors' as we would call them today, used her trial to capture the newspaper headlines at a time when they might have disclosed the failure of a French offensive and that their army was close to mutiny. It has been suggested that Mata Hari was executed more on the need to boost French morale than any sense of justice.

Trebitsch Lincoln

Few have led a more adventurous or debauched life than Trebitsch Lincoln. Born Ignatz Trebitsch in Hungary in 1879, he came from a family of shipbuilders who were devout Jews. After failing as a journalist and being wanted by the police for theft, he left his homeland and settled in Germany and there married and converted to Christianity. He next arrived in Britain where he worked in missions in Bristol and London before, again suspected of theft, he left for Canada where he was ordained an Anglican deacon by the Bishop of Montreal. On his return to Britain he was appointed curate at the parish of Applemore in Kent but, rejected by his parishioners, he left for London and took the name Trebitsch Lincoln. In London, he was introduced to David Lloyd George who recommended him for employment as a researcher to Seebohm Rowntree, the eminent sociologist. In 1909, after borrowing £10,000 from his employer, Lincoln urged Rowntree to back him as the Liberal candidate in the general election of that year. With a slender majority of only 30, he was returned to Westminster as the Member for Darlington.

137
the propaganda war –
spies and espionage

13

In Parliament, he made a fool of himself and in the next general election, he was not even adopted as a candidate. Back in London, he looked for work but when Rowntree pressed for the repayment of his loan, he left for the United States and there he made a number of anti-British speeches and offered to spy for the German intelligence services. The British government demanded his extradition and on his arrival back in London he was arrested, deprived of his British citizenship and deported. However, this only seemed to encourage Lincoln's bizarre behaviour. After the war, he became involved in German politics and then moved to Czechoslovakia but was expelled from both countries for stealing money. In 1921, he made his way to China, there converted to Buddhism and became a Buddhist monk. Five years later, he returned to London to visit his son, a soldier serving in the British army, who had been sentenced to death for murder. Afterwards he travelled the world as a self-styled 'ambassador of peace' but got into trouble for raping a nun. It is said that he spent the rest of his life living in a YMCA hostel in Shanghai and died there in 1943.

Sigmund Georgievich Rosenblum

Born at Odessa in Russia, Sigmund Georgievich Rosenblum was the son of a colonel in the Russian army. After discovering that he was illegitimate, he stowed away on a ship bound for South America and there followed a variety of jobs. Able to speak six different languages, he began to work for the British Secret Service on a freelance basis. He took the name Sidney Reilly and during the war often worked on his own initiative. During the time that he was employed as a welder in the Krupps armaments factory in Germany and later for a firm of German shipbuilders, he stole important plans that he passed to Britain. It is possible that he was working for Russian and American intelligence at the same time. In 1917 he joined the Royal Flying Corps and worked behind the German lines gathering information for the Allies and calculating how close Germany was to defeat. For these missions, he was awarded the Military Cross. The end of the war did not bring an end to his espionage activities. Sent to Russia to spy on Lenin's Communist government, he was eventually caught and executed in November 1925. However there are rumours that suggest that he was still alive in 1927.

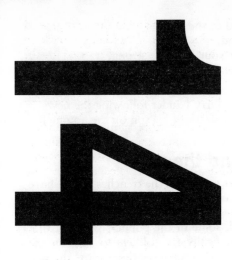

14

music, poetry and art of the First World War

'Keep right on to the end of the road,
  Keep right on to the end,
Tho the way be long, let your heart be strong,
  Keep right on to the bend.'

(From a song, *Keep Right on to the End of the Road*,
written by Sir Harry Lauder following the news
of the death of his son on the Somme)

Popular music and the war

During the war, few soldiers serving in the trenches would have shown much interest in cultural niceties but would have been far more attracted to popular songs and the ribald music-hall humour of the day. Indeed, some of the popular songs of that time were not written specifically for soldiers to sing on the march but had been in circulation for some time before the war began. In addition, soldiers sang parodies of their own creation based on popular songs and even hymns, and they were often extremely crude.

Although born in the Midlands in England, Jack Judge, a prolific songwriter, had Irish parents and he indicated the love of the land of his ancestors when he wrote *It's A Long Way To Tipperary*. The song became famous when a Daily Mail reporter mentioned that the soldiers of the original BEF sang the tune when they first arrived in France in 1914. Two songs were combined to produce the soldiers' favourite *Mademoiselle From Armentières*. As was the case with most popular songs, the versions sung by the soldiers were extremely vulgar and unprintable. In reality, the *mademoiselle* referred to in the song was an extremely virtuous young French girl. *Pack Up Your Troubles In Your Old Kit Bag* first came to notice when it won a marching-song competition in 1915 but shortly afterwards the composer, George Asaf, took his own life in a fit of depression. Clifford Grey's *If You Were The Only Girl In The World* was written in 1916 and still retains some popularity today. In the same year Ivor Novello wrote *Keep The Home Fires Burning*, and *Take Me Back To Dear Old Blighty* first appeared. 'Blighty' was the name given by the British troops to home. After the American entry into the war in 1917, the songs of George M. Cohen became very popular particularly *Over There* and *Yankee Doodle Dandy*. With most songs, it was usually the case that the chorus became more popular than the song itself and the most popular parodies sung loudly in barrack rooms and *estaminets* were based upon the marches *Colonel Bogey* and *Blaze Away* and such hymns as *O God Our Help In Ages Past*:

> John Wesley had a little dog,
> he was so very thin.
> He took him to the Gates of Hell
> and threw the bastard in.

Entertainers

Born in 1870 and the son of a colliery worker, one of the great music-hall entertainers was Harry Lauder and he became one of the most famous and highest paid singer-comedians of his day. A friend of royalty and American presidents, his most popular songs included *I Love A Lassie, Roamin' In The Gloaming* and *A Wee Deoch-and-Doruis* - a 'Deoch-and-Doruis' is a farewell drink. On New Year's Day 1917 he received news that his son had been killed in action. Later Lauder wrote a song that reflected his own personal grief and his determination to encourage others to carry on – *Keep Right On To The End Of The Road*. He went to France and with others entertained troops close to the front line or as he put it 'to sing to the boys in the thick of the trouble'. He even complained that his singing was spoiled by the noise of the guns. In Britain, he used his music-hall act to support the recruitment campaign and it is said that as a result of his efforts over 12,000 men joined up. He also set up a fund for wounded servicemen and in 1919 was awarded a knighthood for his contribution to the war effort.

Most army units contained men with experience as entertainers and they were used to form concert parties. The war also touched the lives of many other entertainers. Basil Hallam, a popular music-hall comedian best known for his song *Gilbert the Filbert* was killed in an accident when leaving an observation balloon. The actors Basil Rathbone and Ronald Colman both served in the war as did B. C. Hilliam, one of a music-hall double act known as 'Flotsam and Jetsam' and Chesney Allen of 'Crazy Gag' fame. The comedians Max Miller and Tommy Handley, later to win greater fame during the Second World War, were both serving soldiers until they joined concert parties. In addition, scores of sportsmen, international footballers, cricketers and rugby players joined up and many lost their lives in the war.

The war poets

Why did the First World War produce so many poets? Was it
that some men used verse to give voice to their patriotism? Did
some use verse to protest against their experiences in the
trenches and the blood-letting and carnage of the war or did
their wartime experiences heighten their perception? Were some
exhilarated by it all? To what extent did the often static nature
of trench warfare give them time to collect their thoughts and
set them down in verse and were their poems really prayers
begging for it all to stop? With only a few did their initial
patriotism endure and for Wilfred Owen and others it became
necessary to challenge the 'old lie' that 'it is sweet and noble to
die for one's country'. Some, like A. E. Housman, turned their
anger on God for allowing such things to happen and not
bringing an end to the suffering. In Britain, some publishers
rejected poems thought to be unpatriotic or likely to undermine
the nation's morale and for this reason many poets did not have
their works published until the war was over.

Among the most popular poets of the First World War were
Rupert Brooke, Wilfred Owen, Siegfried Sassoon and John
McCrae but there were also many others. Not all were officers
or educated men but they were all able to express their feelings
in verse. These included Leslie Coulson, a sergeant in the Royal
Fusiliers, killed in action in 1916; Wilfred Gibson, a former
social worker from London's East End; the scholars Edmund
Blunden, A. E. Housman and Robert Graves; the British Prime
Minister's son, Raymond Asquith; and W. N. Hodgson who died
on the Somme. The works of the Irish MP and lawyer
T. M. Kettle were considered by some to be second only to Owen
whilst the Welshman, Ellis Humphrey Evans, won the chair at
the Welsh National Eisteddfod in 1918. At the ceremony, it was
announced that he had been killed in action a few months earlier
and the crowd stood in silence as the chair was draped in black.

Of the popular poets, Rugby and Cambridge educated Rupert
Brooke was commissioned in the Royal Naval Division and on
his way to Gallipoli in 1915, he was taken ill and died of food
poisoning. He was buried on the Greek island of Skyros. His
poem, *The Soldier*, was indicative of his patriotic spirit:

> If I should die, think only this of me:
>   That there's some corner of a foreign field
> That is forever England

In spite of his ill health, Oswestry-born Wilfred Owen was
commissioned in the Manchester Regiment. After being invalided

home, he returned to the Western Front and was awarded the Military Cross for bravery but he was killed a week before the end of the war. In his *Anthem For Doomed Youth* he wrote:

> What passing bells for those who die as cattle?
>   Only the monstrous anger of the guns,
> Only the stuttering rifles' rapid rattle
>   Can patter out their hasty orisons.
> No mockeries for them from prayers or bells,
>   Nor any voice of mourning save the choirs –

Most critical of the waste of human lives was Siegfried Sassoon who served in the Royal Welsh Fusiliers and had earlier won the Military Cross. In *Attack*, he describes the horrors of war unsparingly:

> Lines of grey, muttering faces, masked with fear,
>   They leave their trenches, going over the top,
> While time ticks blank and busy on their wrists,
>   And hope, with furtive eyes and grappling fists,
> Flounders in mud. Jesus, make it stop!

> Copyright Siegfried Sassoon by kind permission of
> George Sassoon

The Canadian doctor, John McCrae, wrote one of the most famous poems of the war, *In Flanders Fields*:

> In Flanders fields the poppies blow
>   Between the crosses, row on row,
> They mark our place, and in the sky
>   The larks, still bravely singing, fly
> Scarce heard amid the guns below.

Not all poets expressed themselves with patriotic fervour or in terms of disillusionment. Some used humour laced with satire to illustrate the impact of the war on the minds of sick and confused men and none did this better than Wilfred Gibson:

> Both his legs are shot away,
>   And his head is light,
> So he keeps muttering
>   All the blessed night
>
> Two rows of cabbages,
> Two of curly greens,
> Two rows of early peas,
> Two of kidney beans.
>
> (From *In the Ambulance*
>   by Wilfred Gibson)

> Neck-deep in mud
>   He mowed and raved –
> He who braved
>   The field of blood –
> And as a lad
>   Just out of school
> Yelled – April Fool!
> And laughed like mad.
>
> (From *Mad* by Wilfred Gibson)

Saddest of all was the fate of the British Gloucester-born poet and composer Ivor Gurney who, after being wounded and then gassed in 1917, was discharged and then spent the last 15 years of his life in a mental asylum suffering from schizophrenia. Amongst his most famous works were two collections of poems, *Severn* and *Somme*.

War artists and cartoonists

Although less well known, the works of some of the artists of the First World War matched that of the poets in their extent and variety. Again like the poets, some used their work to illustrate the unswerving loyalty of the soldier and expose the harsh realities of war. The brothers Paul and John Nash were amongst the most famous of the war artists and both served in the trenches and were deeply influenced by their experiences there. Their paintings include Paul Nash's *We Are Making A New World*, a derisive title for a work showing the devastation of war and John Nash's *Over The Top* that depicts a real-life event in the history of his own regiment, the Artists' Rifles. The brothers were eventually appointed official war artists. Paintings that were considered to be amongst the most true to life were those of Eric Kennington who was later discharged from the army as medically unfit. Other war artists included Colin Gill, Frank Dobson, Augustus John, F. H. Varley, a Canadian, and the New Zealander, W. B. Wollen.

Unlike poets and artists, the work of cartoonists was circulated in newspapers and magazines and brought them immediate recognition. The outstanding cartoonist of the war was Bruce Bairnsfather. Born in India and the son of an army officer, in 1911 he was commissioned into the Royal Warwickshire Regiment but resigned in order to attend art school. At the start of the war Bairnsfather rejoined his former regiment and was sent to France. Many of his cartoons appeared in the magazine *Bystander* and his most famous cartoon character was 'Old Bill', a soldier with a walrus moustache who invariably wore a scarf and balaclava. Although his cartoons were immensely popular and won him a worldwide reputation, there were those in the High Command who thought his work offensive. They described 'Old Bill' as a 'vulgar caricature of our heroes in the trenches' and asked for Bairnsfather's work to be banned. After the war he continued to draw cartoons and during the Second World War served as the official cartoonist to the United States army in Europe. Other popular cartoonists included Bernard Partridge who worked for the magazine *Punch* and Frank Reynolds.

145
music, poetry and art
of the First World War
14

The cinema

Even though the first public showing of moving films had occurred in the Empire Theatre, Leicester Square in 1896 and films had been made about the Boer War, at the start of the war British cinematography was still in its infancy. Against the wishes of Kitchener, newsreel films were made that recorded some of the early events on the Western Front and in 1916 came the first feature length documentary, *The Battle of the Somme*. The film, made by two cameramen, Geoffrey Malins and J. B. McDowell, showed the great bombardment that preceded the offensive, men 'going over the top' and the return of the wounded and the dead. Although audiences were shocked by some of the scenes of suffering and death, they thought the film impressive and public reaction was generally favourable. Widely distributed across the country, a private showing was arranged for the Royal Family at Windsor but there were those opposed to the showing of the film and the Dean of Durham protested 'against an entertainment which wounds the hearts and violates the very sanctity of bereavement'. Others complained that the film was diminished by supporting programmes that included comedies and cartoons. Later, the impact of the film was lessened when it was revealed that some sequences were filmed away from the front line and even staged in Britain. Nevertheless, at the time the film had a profound effect on wartime cinema-going audiences.

15

1917 – enter the United States; exit Russia

This chapter will cover:
- the decision of the Germans to resort to unrestricted submarine warfare
- the impact of the Zimmermann telegram
- the significance of the entry of the United States into the war
- the later events on the Russian front
- the events leading to a revolution in Russia in March 1917
- the October Revolution and the Bolshevik takeover and the decision to seek an armistice.

Over there, over there,
  Send the word, send the word over there –
The Yanks are coming,
  The Yanks are coming,
The drums rum-tuming
  Everywhere

(From a song, *Over There*, written by
George M. Cohen in 1917)

The American situation

Decades of emigration to the United States meant that the
majority of Americans could trace their ancestral roots back to
Europe. They were the direct descendants of those who had
reached America from Britain, France, Germany, Italy, Russia
and every other European country and cultural ties with their
countries of origin remained strong. Although there were over
6 million Americans of German descent, the closest ties were
with Great Britain and together they represented the world's
two greatest English-speaking nations. For obvious reasons,
Americans of British, French, Italian and Russian origin
favoured the Allies whilst those of German and Austrian descent
did their utmost to ensure that the United States remained
neutral. Remember too that Irish immigrants to America were
unlikely to back any measures likely to benefit Britain. Many
Americans who continued to support their country's traditional
isolationist stand were against any involvement in a European
war and saw no good reason why their husbands and sons
should give their lives in a war being fought in the interests of
British, French and German imperialism. They saw it as a
European conflict and thought that Europeans should be left to
settle their own differences.

At the start of the hostilities, Woodrow Wilson, the American
president, declared his country's intention to remain neutral. In
reality, from the very beginning of the war the United States had
been making a vital contribution to the Allied war effort.
American industrialists quickly discovered that the war offered
them lucrative business opportunities and between 1914 and
1916 there was virtually an unrestricted flow of war materials
across the Atlantic Ocean. As American exports to the Allies
increased fourfold, so their economy enjoyed a major boom.
Undoubtedly many American arms manufacturers would have
been equally happy to trade with Germany but the Royal Navy
made that impossible. The war also benefited the United States
in other ways since it provided the opportunity for their country

to draw ahead of their major trading rivals, Britain and Germany, and the years 1914–18 helped to lay the foundations of America's future economic prosperity.

American entry into the war

From the early months of the war Allied propagandists had worked tirelessly to sour relations between the United States and Germany. With easy access to the media, pro-British spokesmen were able to stir up anti-German sentiment and the fact that Germany had declared war on both Russia and France and then invaded neutral Belgium was exploited to the full. Following the invasion of Belgium and lurid accounts in the American press of German atrocities against the civilian population, the Allies found it relatively easy to cultivate the image of the 'Beastly Hun'. Many stories were greatly exaggerated and some were totally untrue. Germany, on the other hand, did not handle her relations with the United States with any great sensitivity and played into the hands of the Allies when Germans committed outrages that incensed American public opinion. In 1915, the German image was further tarnished when a U-boat sank the British liner, *Lusitania*. News that there were 128 Americans amongst those drowned led to a wave of anti-German hysteria and there were widespread demands for a declaration of war. Little was made of the fact that the German embassy in Washington had placed a notice in the press warning that 'travellers sailing in the war zone on the ships of Great Britain or her allies do so at their own risk'. The Germans also claimed that the vessel had been carrying war materials amongst her cargo, a claim that has never been totally disproved. The outrage subsided when the Kaiser placated American public opinion by giving an undertaking that German submarines would not again sink passenger liners. Soon afterwards, came the execution of the British nurse, Edith Cavell, even though Woodrow Wilson had been among the world leaders that had asked for her life to be spared. Once again, anti-German propagandists had a field day.

The ongoing issue of unrestricted submarine warfare

As the war progressed, it became increasingly difficult for the Germans to remain indifferent to the fact that large amounts of war materials and foodstuffs were reaching British ports on board neutral shipping, much of it American. This unrestricted flow of goods across the Atlantic went some way towards countering the effects of the German U-boat campaign against the British Isles. Conscious of the need to avoid further damaging relations with the United States, Kaiser Wilhelm had resisted pressure from Ludendorff and the German High Command to impose a total blockade on Britain. However, with no sign of victory on the Western Front, national survival became a major issue and the Germans became less concerned at the prospect of provoking America. Anyway, many Germans maintained that the United States had already taken sides in the war. Finally, in January 1917, the Kaiser gave way to pressure and declared unrestricted submarine warfare so that the ships of any nationality found in waters around the British Isles and off the coast of France became liable to be sunk without warning. The United States immediately severed diplomatic relations with Germany as did a number of Latin American countries including Brazil, Bolivia and Peru. From a German viewpoint, it was a high-risk gamble. On the one hand, the sinking of American ships and the loss of American lives would almost certainly bring the United States into the war; on the other hand, six months of unrestricted submarine warfare might be sufficient to bring Britain and France to their knees and allow Germany to win the war. In spite of these events, in 1916 Woodrow Wilson managed to win re-election as president under the slogan, 'He Kept Us Out Of The War'. Back in the White House, he made every effort to bring about peace by offering to mediate between the Allies and the Central Powers by asking both sides to accept 'a peace between equals ... a peace without victory'. His pleas fell on deaf ears and his efforts came to nothing. As German submarines began to sink an increasing number of American merchant ships, a declaration of war seemed only a matter of time. In February 1917, the British liner *Laconia* was torpedoed in the Atlantic with a further loss of American lives and a week later news of the contents of the Zimmermann telegram appeared in American newspapers.

The Zimmermann telegram

In January 1917, a secret communication sent by the German Foreign Minister, Arthur Zimmermann, to the German envoy in Mexico was intercepted and deciphered by British naval intelligence and the following month its contents were made known to the American government. The telegram suggested that the envoy should approach the Mexican government with a proposal of an alliance between the two countries. In the event of the American entry into the war, the telegram offered Mexico German military aid to support their invasion of the United States in order to reclaim the lost states of New Mexico, Texas and Arizona. The telegram went on to hint that Germany would also do her utmost to encourage Japan to change sides and attack American naval bases in the Pacific. Immediately, the German ambassador in Washington, Count Johan von Bernstorff, denounced the telegram as a fake, a crude ploy by the British to involve the United States in the war. Bernstorff, who had an American wife, had made himself popular with Woodrow Wilson by supporting the need for a negotiated peace. Unfortunately, his reputation with the American people was tarnished by his lifestyle and with few able to take him seriously, he became something of a laughing stock. A ladies' man and keen party-goer, a photograph of him surrounded by bathing beauties appeared in the press and this undermined his influence both in America and Germany. With anti-German feeling already running high, the Zimmermann telegram proved the last straw. On 2 April 1917, President Wilson appeared before a specially convened meeting of Congress and said:

> 'With a profound sense of the solemn and even tragic character of the step I am taking and of the grave responsibilities which it involves, I advise that Congress declare that the recent course of the Imperial German Government to be nothing less than war against the Government and people of the United States … It is a fearful thing to lead this great peaceful people into war … America is privileged to spend her blood and might on the principles that gave her birth…'

His audience applauded loudly and four days later, on 6 April 1917, the United States declared war on Germany. His conduct viewed with great displeasure by the Kaiser and the German military, Bernstoff was recalled to Berlin.

The Russian situation

> 'Russia loves to feel the whip. It's their nature … Be Peter the Great, Ivan the Terrible … crush them all under you.'
>
> (Alexandra, Tsarina and wife of Nicholas II, in a letter to her husband in 1916)

As we have seen, during the early stages of the war Russia experienced mixed fortunes on the Eastern Front. Limited successes in East Prussia and Galicia turned to disaster when the brave but ill-equipped and inadequately-trained Russian soldiers proved no match for the superior firepower of the Germans. By the end of 1914, the Russian armies were totally demoralized and at the point of collapse. At this point Tsar Nicholas II decided to take over command of his armies but although well intended it was a foolhardy act since the Tsar could now be personally held responsible for any disaster that followed. It was also a decision that meant that he spent most of his time away from Petrograd at his army headquarters at Mogliev and was unavailable to exercise full control over events on the home front. In the Russian capital, these responsibilities fell largely to the Tsarina and her trusted councillor, Gregory Rasputin, and on the advice of this disreputable priest, she encouraged her husband to appoint corrupt and incompetent men to important posts in the government. Being German by birth, the Russian people distrusted Alexandra and even though such rumours were unfounded, some even went as far as to suggest that she was a spy. Then, in December 1916, Rasputin was murdered and the distraught Tsarina found herself with no confidante to turn to for advice.

The Eastern Front during 1916 and 1917

When General Alexey Brusilov launched a major offensive against their positions in the summer of 1916, it took the Germans and Austrians by complete surprise. The Russians broke through the Austrian lines and caused sufficient panic for the Germans to withdraw troops from the Western Front to reinforce their allies. The Russian advance into Galicia also encouraged Romania, long sympathetic to the Allies, to enter the war. Brusilov's offensive led to the capture of 375,000 prisoners and was to prove the only really successful Russian campaign of the war. Unfortunately, without adequate supplies and reinforcements, Brusilov could not sustain the momentum of his advance and a strong German counteroffensive again forced his armies to retreat and the episode ended in their rout. From a Russian point of view, the Brusilov offensive represented a last throw of the dice. With a casualty rate now running into millions and the economic situation at home at crisis point, exhaustion and disillusionment among the Tsar's soldiers turned first to desperation and then finally mutiny. The peasant soldiers and their families had suffered enough and the scene was set for revolution.

The revolution of March 1917

The threat of revolution was not new to the Russian situation. Numerous radical political groups had appeared during the latter half of the nineteenth and early twentieth centuries of which the most important were the Populists, the Octobrists, the Social Revolutionaries and the Social Democrats, a party dedicated to the communist theories of Karl Marx. In 1903, differences within the party led the Social Democrats to split into Bolsheviks and Mensheviks. The Bolsheviks, the faction most dedicated to revolution as a means of ridding Russia of tsarist rule, was led by Vladimir Ulyanov, better known to the world as Lenin. In 1905, following defeat in a war against Japan, Russia came close to revolution and Nicholas was only able to restore the situation by making concessions that included the promise of a more democratic constitution and an elected government or Duma. The Tsar might have achieved more and averted the difficulties that were to follow had he been even more conciliatory and shown a greater willingness to collaborate with the Duma. It proved to be a lost opportunity and instead Nicholas went back on his word and continued to rule as an autocrat. When Russia entered the war in 1914, the country was swept by a wave of patriotic fervour and the Tsar appeared to have the backing of his people but by 1917 this had disappeared.

During the third winter of the war the situation worsened as inflation led to rising prices and food and fuel shortages became acute. There were mass demonstrations, rioters took to the streets to loot bakeries and food shops and strikes hit public transport and prevented the publication of newspapers. With the collapse of law and order, effective government became first difficult and then impossible. Heavy losses at the front had drained the Russian army of its regular soldiers and these had been replaced by embittered peasant conscripts whose loyalty was questionable. To add to their misery, the winter of 1916–17 was bitterly cold even by Russian standards with temperatures falling to 35 degrees below zero. As men threw away their weapons, disobeyed their officers and deserted, so soldiers made their way home and the country edged towards open revolution. Rodzianko, the president of the Duma, telegraphed the Tsar and begged him to return to Petrograd. He warned, 'The situation is growing worse. Measures should be taken as tomorrow may be too late.' Nicholas commented, 'That fat bellied Rodzianko has written me a lot of nonsense that I won't even bother to answer' and then he ordered the disorders in the capital city to be put down by force. Immediately the whole country was paralysed by a general strike as public buildings were set on fire, inmates released from prisons and instead of taking action against the demonstrators, the soldiers joined them. It was obvious that a dramatic upheaval was imminent. In an attempt to restore order, Nicholas left the front and made his way home. On the way to Petrograd, his train was stopped and his military commanders advised him that the situation in Petrograd was out of control and that he had no choice but to abdicate. The Tsar offered to abdicate in favour of his younger brother Grand Prince Michael but after some hesitation, the prince wisely declined the offer and so Russia became a republic. Following the March Revolution, a Provisional Government was set up under the leadership of Prince Lvov, a liberal. The new government promised to call a general election and establish a system of democratic government. During these upheavals, the Germans made no moves on the Eastern Front since they were confident that the new government would ask for peace. Unfortunately, the Provisional Government made a disastrous decision when, under pressure from Britain and France, it decided that Russia should remain loyal and continue in the war.

The October Revolution – the end

The Provisional Government was not in control of events since it had to share power with the influential workers' council, the Petrograd Soviet. Acting on its own initiative, the Petrograd Soviet issued an order that soldiers were to obey the instructions of the Soviet and this move led to the final breakup of the Russian army. News of events in Russia reached Lenin, who was living in exile in Switzerland, and the German High Command took steps to ensure that the Bolshevik leader was able to return home as soon as possible. Smuggled across Germany in a sealed railway carriage, on his arrival back in Petrograd a huge crowd gave Lenin a tumultuous reception. Using the slogan 'Peace, bread and land', the Bolshevik leader demanded that the war should be brought to an immediate end and all power handed to the Soviets. During the weeks that followed, Russia was in chaos and news of further defeats on the battlefield led to fresh outbreaks of unrest. The Provisional Government blamed Lenin for the setbacks and accused him of being in the pay of the Germans. Under threat of arrest, he fled to Finland. Meanwhile, the leadership of the Provisional Government passed from Lvov to Alexander Kerensky, a moderate socialist. The new leader faced an immediate challenge to his authority when General Lavr Kornilov, with the backing of other military leaders as well as businessmen and industrialists, attempted to overthrow the government. Kerensky played into the hands of the Bolsheviks when he asked for their help to resist Kornilov's attempted coup. With Lenin back in Petrograd, the Bolsheviks made their final plans to seize power. When it came on 24/25 October, there was little resistance and the takeover of the capital was accomplished with little bloodshed. The following month, Lenin ordered the Russian armies to stop fighting and declared his readiness to open negotiations with the Germans. When the delegates met at Brest-Litovsk, the leader of the Bolshevik delegation, Leon Trotsky, tried to delay agreement by refusing to accept the terms. Their patience exhausted, the German army resumed its advance towards Petrograd until Lenin instructed his representative to accept any terms demanded no matter how harsh.

As you can imagine, the Russian withdrawal from the conflict came as a great disappointment to the Allies who went as far as to offer support to the new Bolshevik regime in return for their continued participation in the war. In the long run, Germany too was a loser since the end of the war on the Eastern Front meant that thousands of prisoners of war were allowed to return home taking with them new and dangerous revolutionary ideas. As we shall see, their influence was to become all too apparent in Germany during the final stages of the war.

16 the war against the Turks

This chapter will cover:
- the nature and extent of the Turkish Empire
- the Armenian massacres
- British campaigns in Mesopotamia and the siege of Kut-el-Amara
- the Palestine campaign
- Lawrence and the Arab revolt.

They shall not return to us, the resolute and young,
   The eager and whole-hearted whom we gave:
But the men who left them thriftily to lie in their own dung,
   Shall they come with years if honour to the grave?'

(From the poem *Mesopotamia*
by Rudyard Kipling, 1865–1936)

The Turkish Empire

The entry of Turkey into the war in 1914 provided Germany
with an ally well placed to harass the Allies on several fronts. So
far, we have only considered one aspect of the war against the
Turks – the Dardanelles campaign – but the Allies, particularly
the British and Imperial troops had to fight bitterly-contested
campaigns against them elsewhere. Although the Turks had
virtually been expelled from Europe, they still controlled a large
empire in the Middle East that extended from the Dardanelles

figure 18 the extent of the Turkish Empire

in the west to the Persian Gulf in the east and from the Black Sea in the north to the Gulf of Aden in the south. It had common borders with both the Russian Caucasus and British-controlled Egypt. Dissident Arabs keen to win their independence and freedom after centuries of Turkish rule populated much of the area. The proximity of Turkey to the Suez Canal meant that they were able to threaten Britain's all-important sea links with India as well as Australia and New Zealand and they were also well within striking distance of the British-financed oilfields at the head of the Persian Gulf. As the British and ANZACs had discovered at Gallipoli, the Turks were formidable fighting soldiers. Even so, the rulers of the Turkish Empire had problems of their own. Within the borders of Turkey, the largely Christian Armenians were pressing for autonomy whilst to the south in Palestine and Mesopotamia, the Arab peoples longed to rid themselves of their Turkish masters. In addition, Turkey was an economically-backward country with little industry and inadequate road and rail communications. Militarily, its armies depended heavily on German armaments and leadership.

The Armenian massacres

In December 1914, the Turkish War Minister, Enver Pasha, ordered the invasion of the Russian Caucasus with the intention of threatening the important Baku oilfields. The high mountain ranges made campaigning extremely difficult and the badly-equipped Turkish troops, unused to the severity of a Russian winter, suffered great hardship. Early in 1915, the Turks were forced to retreat and then found themselves facing the threat of invasion when Russian forces crossed the border into Armenia, a province in north-west Turkey. Armenians, largely Christian by religion and strongly influenced by western culture, had long been a thorn in the side of the Turks. The Armenians demanded self-rule that was contrary to the ambitions of the nationalist Young Turk movement who wanted to create an even greater Turkish Empire stretching as far east as Samarkand. At the time of the Russian invasion in 1915 the Turkish government accused the Armenians of collaborating with the invaders and they took their revenge by planning an act of genocide aimed at exterminating the Armenian people, a measure we would refer to today as 'ethnic cleansing'. The slaughter began in Constantinople where the leaders of the Armenian community were thrown from ships and drowned. The brutalities then continued across Turkey and Armenia where Armenian men, women and children were deported, tortured, starved and butchered and their wealth expropriated. In some areas men were forced to dig their own graves before being shot and women were given the choice of embracing Islam or death. It has been estimated that 1.5 million Armenians were murdered and a further 1 million deported. Some escaped by struggling across the mountains and seeking refuge in Russia. Whilst the German commander of the Turkish army, Liman von Sanders, condoned the slaughter, other military leaders, including Ludendorff, strongly disapproved.

The Allied campaign in Mesopotamia

Mesopotamia, modern-day Iraq, is the region that surrounds and embraces the Rivers Tigris and Euphrates. In 1914, a force of British and Indian troops was sent to the area to safeguard the oil installations at Ahwaz on the Persian Gulf and deal with any possible Turkish threat to the Suez Canal. The force landed at Shatt-al-Arab, the point where the Rivers Tigris and Euphrates converge, where they found Turkish resistance weak.

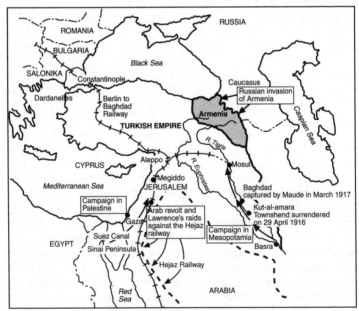

figure 19 campaigns fought against the Turks in Mesopotamia

This encouraged the force, commanded by Major General Sir Charles Townshend, to proceed inland by boat along the River Tigris and once the town of Kut-al-Amara had been taken, the expedition moved overland towards Baghdad. Short of supplies and faced by strengthening Turkish resistance, the British and Indian advance came to a halt at Ctesiphon and they were forced to retrace their steps back to Kut.

Kut-al-Amara lies 800 kilometres (497 miles) upstream from Basra at the head of the Persian Gulf. It was here that the Turks, commanded by the German general, Kolmar Von Der Goltz, besieged Townshend's force of 10,000 men for five terrible months from November 1915 to April 1916. By day, the men suffered from the sweltering heat but at night the temperatures cooled to near freezing. In such a climate, the men were forced to endure appalling hardship and as medical supplies dwindled so cases of malaria and dysentery reached epidemic proportions. At first, Townshend was promised early relief and he felt able to keep the garrison on full daily food rations. Sadly the promised relief did not materialize and there was an acute shortage of food which meant that the 2,000 mules and 3,000 horses had to be slaughtered so that their flesh became the staple diet. A soldier wrote 'We have horse steak, horse steak and kidney pie, horse olives, horse mince, horse rissoles, potted horse, horse soup, stuffed horse heart and horse liver'. Indian soldiers suffered additionally since they refused to eat horse flesh. Meanwhile, disheartened by three failed attempts to relieve the town, the defenders of Kut rallied and managed to beat off a series of fierce attacks. With approval from higher command, Townshend asked the Turks for a six-day armistice and their commander, Khalil Pasha, agreed providing talks were held between the two sides. At the talks, Khalil demanded the unconditional surrender of the garrison. Townshend, now of the opinion that any future resistance would be futile, destroyed everything of value in the town and ordered the white flag to be hoisted. The surrender of the British and Indian defenders of Kut was one of the worst military defeats ever inflicted on the British army and added to the damage already done to British prestige at Gallipoli the previous year.

For the survivors of the siege, even worse was to follow. The emaciated and diseased men of the garrison were made to undertake a forced march into captivity during which they were savagely beaten or killed in acts of wanton brutality so that of the 13,000 British and Indian captives some 5,000 were murdered or died from maltreatment. Meanwhile Townshend himself was well treated and lived in comfortable, if isolated, captivity in a villa on the shore of the Black Sea. Little wonder the military historian John Keegan has described him as 'a bad general and no gentleman' (*Who's Who in Military History*, 1967).

Townshend's replacement as British commander in Mesopotamia was Sir Stanley Maude. After careful planning, he advanced on Kut and recaptured the town on Christmas Eve 1916 before moving against and capturing the city of Baghdad. In November 1917, Maude, who had earlier been taken ill, died of cholera and his place was taken by Lieutenant General Marshall. It was not until the autumn of 1918 that the oilfields at Baku and Mosul were finally taken and the campaign in Mesopotamia finally came to an end.

The Palestine campaign

Early in 1915, a 20,000-strong Turkish army crossed the Sinai Peninsula and advanced on the Suez Canal, said to be 'the lifeline of the British Empire'. British forces, under the command of General Sir Archibald Murray, easily repelled their attempted invasion of Egypt and by the end of the year had themselves moved forward from Egypt to the borders of Palestine. Even though they built a road and water pipeline as they advanced, Murray's attempt to capture the town of Gaza ended in failure and General Sir Edmund Allenby was sent to replace him. Nicknamed 'The Bull', Allenby was an ill-tempered and outspoken man who was liable to take to task any inefficient subordinate. In an effort to gain a much-needed morale-boosting victory, Lloyd George urged Allenby to 'take Jerusalem before Christmas'. His forces, strengthened by reinforcements sent from the Western Front, were immediately successful and won a series of impressive victories over the Turks. Beersheba, Gaza and Jaffa all fell to the British in quick succession and on 9 December 1917, Allenby led his victorious troops into Jerusalem. The success of the Allied campaign in Palestine owed much to the fact that the Turks also had to cope with a widespread Arab revolt. This revolt was largely inspired by Colonel T. E. Lawrence, who was soon to become famously known as Lawrence of Arabia.

T. E. Lawrence – leader of the Arab revolt

Thomas Edward Lawrence was born in 1885 at Tremadoc in North Wales. He was the illegitimate son of an Anglo-Irishman, Thomas Chapman, who later changed his name to Lawrence. He studied history at Oxford University and there won a travelling scholarship that allowed him to take part in archaeological explorations in the Middle East. It was during this time that Lawrence came into contact with the Arabs. He came to admire them immensely and learned their language and became fascinated by their history, culture and customs. During the war, he served in army intelligence and because of his mastery of Arabic he was posted to the Arab Bureau at army headquarters in Cairo. When the Arabs rebelled against their Turkish rulers, Lawrence was sent to assess the situation at first hand and first met the Arab ruler, Hussein, and became a firm friend of his son, Feisal. Afterwards, he remained with the Arabs and liaised between their leaders and Allenby. More importantly, he helped to organize attacks on Turkish outposts and on the Hejaz railway, the essential Turkish supply route that ran between Damascus and Medina. Known to the Arabs as *Al Auruns*, Lawrence became an accomplished guerrilla leader and contributed greatly to the success of Allenby's campaign in Palestine. In part, his popularity with the Arabs rested on the fact that in return for their support, he promised them a chance to achieve their independence. A legendary figure, at the end of the war he returned home to popular acclaim as 'Lawrence of Arabia' and was offered the Victoria Cross and a knighthood but declined both. There were those who attempted to belittle Lawrence's achievements by declaring that his efforts were of little real importance to the outcome of the war since his desert campaign was at best 'a sideshow within a sideshow'. In reality, at an important stage in the war in the Middle East, Lawrence's force of some 3,000 Bedouin Arabs tied down over 50,000 Turkish regular troops and as the Arab revolt grew, the Turkish authorities had to deploy over 150,000 troops across the region.

T. E. Lawrence – the enigma

The Arabs had fought with the British on the assumption that once the Turks had been defeated and the war was over, their homeland, Palestine, would become an independent Arab state. Unfortunately, earlier in 1917 the British Foreign Secretary, Arthur Balfour, had declared his country's support for a Jewish national home in Palestine. However, Lawrence's commitment to the Arabs did not end with the armistice in 1918 and wearing traditional Bedouin-style dress, he accompanied the Arab delegation to the post-war peace conferences in Paris. There he argued their case for independence, the issue for which they had fought, but when the Balfour Declaration was confirmed, Lawrence considered the Arabs to have been betrayed. For a time he worked as a special advisor on Arab affairs but disillusioned by his country's Middle East policy, he resigned and made a determined effort to disappear from the limelight and live in obscurity. He first took the name J. M. Ross and joined the RAF as a lowly-ranked aircraftsman but once his identity was revealed, he was hounded by the press and discharged. He next changed his name to T. E. Shaw and joined the Royal Tank Corps but again his true identity was discovered and he left the army to rejoin the RAF. What privacy he had, he used to enjoy his twin pleasures, writing and travelling at speed. He particularly loved racing along the country roads of Dorset on his motorcycle. He retired in 1935 and shortly afterwards, at the age of 45, died following a motorcycle accident. For a time there was speculation that his accident had been contrived and was yet another ploy to escape the limelight. During his lifetime, Lawrence wrote several books the most famous of which was *The Seven Pillars of Wisdom*, his own account of the Arab revolt.

The final defeat of the Turks

A German offensive in the spring of 1918 meant that British reinforcements sent to Palestine had to return to the Western Front. With his army weakened, Allenby had to bide his time before he could renew his campaign against the Turks. In September 1918, he was able to renew his offensive and at the ancient fortress town of Megiddo, referred to as Armageddon in the New Testament, the Allies won a spectacular victory and routed the Turkish armies. The Battle of Megiddo brought about a rapid Turkish collapse and made possible a rapid advance on Damascus and shortly afterwards the capture of Aleppo by Allied mounted troops and Arab tribesmen. At the same time Bulgarian resistance in the Balkans came to an end and this meant that British forces based in Salonika were now free to advance and threaten Constantinople. The Turks had fought well but could no longer match the Allied forces in Mesopotamia and Palestine and so they had no alternative but to sue for peace. On 30 October 1918, an armistice was signed at the port of Mudros on the island of Lemnos in the Adriatic Sea. By the terms of the armistice, the Turks agreed to surrender their remaining garrisons and allow the Allies to control the important waterways, the Dardanelles and the Bosphorus. The war between Turkey and the Allies was finally at an end.

1917 – a year of disasters

This chapter will cover:
- the situation at the start of 1917
- the failure of Nivelle's spring offensive and mutinies in the French army
- the disaster in the mud at Passchendaele
- the Haig controversy
- the disasters on the Italian Front.

'... the blindest slaughter of a blind war.'
(The historian A. J. P. Taylor's view of the Battle
of Passchendaele in 1917)

The situation at the start of 1917

The year 1917 was to prove a most eventful one and a watershed in the history of the First World War. As we have already seen, it was the year during which Germany declared unrestricted submarine warfare, the United States entered the war and the Bolsheviks seized power in Russia and made a separate peace with the Central Powers. In the Middle East it was the year when the disaster at Kut-al-Amara was avenged when British and Empire troops captured Baghdad and advanced on Jerusalem. At sea, it was the year of the Zeebrugge raid. The sacrifices made by the Anglo-French Allies and Germany at Verdun and the Somme during 1916 had left both sides despairing of victory and as the war degenerated into a series of routine slaughters so the morale of the fighting men deteriorated. In Britain, the initial surge of patriotism and the days of volunteers queuing outside recruitment offices eager to

figure 20 Allied offensives on the Western Front during 1917

fight for 'King and Country' had disappeared and now men had to be conscripted. On the Western and Italian Fronts, 1917 was to be a difficult year with the Allies gaining few successes and suffering further disasters with massive loss of life. Still there was a glimmer of hope – in April America had entered the war but how long would it take before her resources of men and armaments would have an impact on the Western Front?

Events on the Western Front

The heavy losses suffered by the Germans during 1916 made it necessary for Ludendorff to reconsider his strategy. In order to better protect his position and shorten his overextended front line, he decided to withdraw to newly-built fortifications that the Germans referred to as the Siegfried Line but were known to the Allies as the Hindenburg Line. With concrete bunkers, well-established machine-gun positions, a maze of barbed-wire entanglements and much improved accommodation for the German soldiers, the new line of defences was impressive. In order to give the soldiers additional protection, the front line was unusually positioned on the reverse slope of hills away from the enemy and to give warning of an impending attack, lookouts were stationed on the crest of the hill. The organized retreat to the new defence line began early in 1917 and as the Germans withdrew, they laid waste the abandoned French villages, destroyed railway lines, contaminated water supplies and booby-trapped houses and farms. Over 125,000 French civilians were forcibly evacuated and made to work elsewhere. Ludendorff wrote, 'The decision to retreat was not reached without much anguish ... but it was necessary for war reasons, we had no choice.' Secure in their new positions, the Germans awaited the next Allied offensive.

In the spring of 1917, in preparation for a major French offensive to the south, the British attacked in the north in the region of Arras. Following the customary bombardment and the heaviest concentration of gas yet used in the war, the infantrymen moved forward against well-defended German positions. After a week of bloody fighting during which they advanced ten kilometres (six miles), the advance floundered and then came to a standstill. The meagre gains cost the British 84,000 casualties and the Germans only 9,000 fewer. It was during this battle that the Canadian Corps under General Sir Julian Byng captured Vimy Ridge after three hours of the most severe hand-to-hand fighting. The ridge was of strategic importance since it overlooked the towns of Lens and Douai.

Nivelle's spring offensive

In mid-April the French attacked on a 60-kilometre (37-mile) front along the River Aisne between Soissons and Reims with the intention of capturing an important ridge along the Chemin des Dames. The French had high hopes of their new commander, Robert Nivelle, who had replaced Joffre in 1916. Nivelle, whose mother was English, spoke his mother's tongue fluently and got on particularly well with the British Prime Minister, Lloyd George. He had earlier enhanced his reputation at Verdun where he had been responsible for the recapture of Fort Douaumont. Considered an energetic general and a clever tactician, it was Nivelle who claimed to have first successfully integrated the use of infantry and artillery in battle. Boasting 'I have a secret', he introduced the concept of a creeping barrage – an artillery barrage behind which the infantry advanced in relative safety. Bristling with confidence, his promise of a quick breakthrough so impressed Lloyd George that he agreed to place the British armies under his command. It was a decision that incensed Haig, a general in whom Lloyd George had long lost faith, and he complained bitterly to both King George V and the War Cabinet but in the end he gave way on the understanding that it was only a temporary arrangement and that the British army retained its separate identity. Security regarding the planned offensive was non-existent since the Germans had captured Nivelle's battle plans during a trench raid and were forewarned of the coming French attack. Even before the offensive began, German aerial reconnaissance had followed French troop movements so that a large number of their tanks were destroyed as they moved into position. The French High Command had doubts and met to decide whether or not the offensive should be cancelled but after some hesitation, Nivelle had his way. When the offensive started, the creeping barrage advanced too quickly and as they crossed no man's land and made their way through the barbed wire, the French infantry was left exposed to withering German machine-gun fire. In addition, French tanks were of such poor quality that not one was able to reach the German lines. After five calamitous days, the French had failed to take their first day objectives and any limited gains made were lost when the Germans counterattacked. Nivelle's offensive proved a total disaster and had dire consequences.

The French army mutinies

Nivelle's debacle resulted in over 130,000 casualties and led to mutinies in the French army. The high casualty rate together with the mismanagement of the campaign led to a collapse of morale and so great was the mood of defeatism that, had it not been for the American entry into the war, the French government might well have been tempted to agree a compromise peace with Germany. As the mutiny spread, groups of men in 54 divisions in the French army refused to obey orders and whilst some deserted, others demonstrated, called for peace, waved red flags, assaulted their officers and even threatened to march on Paris. Behind the scenes, political agitators, communists and anti-war campaigners encouraged their activities. At the height of the crisis, Nivelle was dismissed and replaced by a French general whose reputation still remained intact, Marshal Philippe Pétain, the saviour of Verdun. Pétain restored order and boosted morale with a mixture of rigorous and humanitarian measures. On the one hand, some 23,000 French soldiers were charged and found guilty of mutiny and although only 55 were shot, some of their leaders were transported to the penal colony, Devil's Island. On the other hand, he promised to improve pay and conditions, guaranteed leave and toured army units telling the fighting men that the period of senseless blood-letting was over and that future campaigns would be planned to avoid heavy losses. By mid-June the crisis was over.

June 1917 – Messines Ridge

During the period of the French army mutinies, whole sections of the front line were left undefended and the Allied war strategy was placed at risk but fortunately, the Germans seemed unaware of the crisis and made no effort to take advantage of the situation. Nevertheless, Haig was forced to act and he ordered an assault on Messines Ridge to the south of the Ypres salient. The ridge that had been in German hands since the early months of the war provided the enemy with an uninterrupted view over the British positions. Following a ten-day bombardment, on 7 June 19 mines containing 450 tonnes of explosive were detonated beneath the German positions along the ridge. It is claimed that the explosions could be heard in London. Within a few hours Messines Ridge was in Allied hands. The idea of using mines to destroy the German positions at Messines was the idea of J. Norton Griffiths, an outspoken Member of Parliament and engineer. Some senior officers were opposed to his plan but, as the historian John Giles has written, 'Norton Griffiths cared little about correct military procedure and lost little sleep over anyone who preferred to work strictly according to the rules' (*The Ypres Salient*, 1970). Another interesting legend about the Messines is that one mine failed to detonate and that a large amount of explosives still lies hidden somewhere on the ridge.

The attack on Messines Ridge was masterminded by General Herbert Plumer, a capable commander and one of the few to have been held in high regard by his own men. White moustached, red faced and plump, Plumer was to be the model for the cartoonist David Low's 'Colonel Blimp'. Some historians consider him to have been the best British general of the war and his capture of Messines Ridge proved to be one of the few Allied successes of that year.

The tunnellers

As we have seen, tunnels were dug and mines exploded under German front-line positions at the onset of the Battle of the Somme and at the start of the assault on Messines Ridge. The men who did this exceptionally hazardous work belonged to the Tunnelling Companies of the Royal Engineers and were mainly recruited from coal-mining areas or were men who had formerly been employed in the building of sewers or as 'clay kickers' during the building of the London Underground. So urgently were they needed that they were shipped to the front line with little or no military training. Some were old men already in their sixties but as long as they were capable of hard work and experienced tunnellers, no one questioned their age. In some ways they formed an elite group since, unlike ordinary infantrymen who received one shilling a day, they received six shillings but the risks involved certainly merited this extra payment. Working in close proximity, officers and men were on more familiar terms than would have been allowed in the trenches above. First they dug shafts down into the ground before branching out in tunnels beneath the enemy lines. They worked in four-hour shifts with picks and shovels and as they inched their way forward, they had to stop regularly to prop up the roof with timber supports. The earth that had been removed had to be hidden from the enemy in case it revealed what they were up to and it was placed in sandbags and winched to the surface and disposed of at night. The dangers they faced were similar to those faced by coal miners generally – flooding, roof falls, explosions and carbon-monoxide poisoning. There was also the danger caused by shells exploding above them on the surface, particularly the *camouflets* that were specially designed to cause subsidence and the crunching *Minenwerfters* or 'Minnies' as they were called. The Germans also employed tunnellers and there was always the chance that those digging under the ground might come across each other. This would result in hand-to-hand fighting and a stampede to get out and explode the mine before the others could escape. Both sides used listening devices to detect the tunnelling of the other with the British and French favouring the use of a geophone, which was similar to a doctor's stethoscope. At the end of each shift, tunnellers received a rum ration and once they had completed four days underground they were allowed four days' rest to recover. The high explosive used in the mines was made from ammonal – a mixture of ammonium nitrate and aluminium – and their detonation was spectacular and described by Philip Warner as similar to 'nineteen volcanoes erupting simultaneously' (*Passchendaele*, 1995).

The Third Battle of Ypres

With the breakdown of discipline in the French army still causing anxiety, Haig planned another diversionary offensive in Flanders. The British commander's decision was also influenced by other considerations. He mistakenly believed that German morale was near breaking point and was concerned by a warning given by Admiral Jellicoe that heavy losses of merchant shipping threatened Britain's ability to continue the war. The attack on Messines Ridge was an intended prelude to a major offensive on the Ypres salient and this time Haig passed the responsibility to General Sir Hubert Gough who possessed neither the tactical skill nor the popularity of Plumer. The ultimate aim of the offensive was to capture a plateau some 60 metres (197 feet) high that like Messines was of considerable strategic importance – Passchendaele Ridge. This time the preliminary bombardment lasted for 14 days and was even more intense than that on the first day of the Somme the previous year. Unfortunately, it coincided with the heaviest rainfall experienced in years and the exploding shells destroyed the dikes and culverts used by farmers to drain the swampy terrain. In torrential rain, troops moved forward towards the ridge across an impossible landscape of flooded fields, clinging mud and holes filled with stinking, putrid water. The stench produced by the ooze that was soon to include the decaying remains of men and horses was repulsive and made men feel ill and a senior British officer visiting the battlefield commented, 'Did we really send men to fight in this?' The Germans added to the horror by introducing for the first time the most harrowing form of chemical warfare, mustard gas. The battle took the form of a series of frontal assaults extending over a period of months. After a number of failed attacks, Gough advised Haig to call the offensive off but instead the commander-in-chief passed control of the campaign to Plumer who immediately followed a more cautious approach. Even so, British, Australian and Canadian troops did not take Passchendaele Ridge until early November. From a British point of view, the battle was the most costly and obscene of the whole war: costly because during five months of fighting, the British army suffered a staggering loss of over 240,000 men in order to advance less than eight kilometres (five miles); obscene because the battle was pointless, need not have been fought and had no real justification. Even worse, the Germans easily recaptured the limited amount of land gained when they launched their own offensive in the spring of 1918.

Cambrai – the first major tank action

The horrendous loss of life during the Third Battle of Ypres did not deter Haig and, determined to maintain the pressure on the Germans, he next launched an offensive at Cambrai against a section of the Hindenburg Line. Up to this time, the use of tanks had been sporadic but now in an attempt to gain a major breakthrough, they were used in large numbers for the first time – 434 of them. The Germans were at first taken by surprise and fled as the tanks followed by infantry smashed through their lines. Since 65 tanks were destroyed by enemy action, 73 broke down and 43 were left floundering in the mud, the first use of tanks on such a scale was far from a qualified success. Even though 11,500 German prisoners were taken, the chance of a decisive breakthrough was lost because the British lacked adequate reserves to press home their attack. Nevertheless, tanks had proved themselves capable of flattening barbed wire and forcing German machine gunners to 'waste their energies on the plated hides of machines, rather than the khaki ones of men'. Reinforced by fresh divisions and supported by a storm of gas shells, the Germans counterattacked and regained their lost ground. On this occasion, British casualties totalled 40,000 with a further 6,000 lost as prisoners.

So, a year of failure on the Western Front came to an end. Much had been gambled in Flanders but little or nothing gained and a breakthrough seemed as far away as ever. During his ongoing squabbles with Haig, Lloyd George had asked him not to risk so much in Flanders but instead to make a greater commitment to the Italian Front.

The Haig controversy

Douglas Haig, born in 1861 into a famous Scottish distilling family, was educated at a public school and Oxford University where he failed to get a degree. After Sandhurst, he was commissioned into the 7th Hussars and served in Britain, in India and in South Africa during the Boer War. Within three weeks of their first meeting, he married the Hon. Dorothy Vivian, a lady-in-waiting to Queen Alexandra. At the outbreak of war in 1914, he was a corps commander based in Aldershot and was sent immediately to France. After the First Battle of Ypres, he was promoted to army commander and in December 1915, after much behind-the-scenes intrigue, he replaced Sir John French as commander-in-chief of the British armies on the Western Front.

A controversial figure, opinions of Haig vary enormously. To some, he was responsible for the slaughters on the Somme and at Passchendaele and was considered unimaginative, not open to new ideas and unconcerned by the heavy casualties suffered by his men – 'a flint hearted butcher of his own soldiers'. In *British Butchers and Bunglers of the First World War* (1996), John Laffin, one of his fiercest critics, says of Haig, 'He was the victim of a strange type of intellectual paralysis which made him plan his battles in three phases – first the artillery blazed away for days, then heavily laden infantry went over the top and the cavalry chafed at the bit as they waited to charge through the breach'. Unfortunately, no breach was ever made and they never did charge. Laffin adds, 'Haig ... must not be indicted for incomprehension but for willful blunders and wicked butchery. There can never be forgiveness.' In *With a Machine Gun to Cambrai* (1969), George Coppard comments on Haig's aloofness, 'He was so completely remote from the actual fighting that he was merely a name, a figurehead.' The Prime Minister, David Lloyd George, who profoundly distrusted Haig and most of the other generals, once referred to him as 'brilliant to the top of his army boots' and in his *War Memoirs* (1936) wrote of Haig that he was 'a painstaking soldier with a sound intelligence of secondary quality'. Lloyd George deplored the field marshal's conventional approach to warfare, his blind faith in repetitive frontal assaults that were proving so costly and his failure to recognize and exploit opportunities. For his part, Haig disliked Lloyd George and did his best to prevent him and other politicians from interfering in military matters. He regarded them as amateurs and out of their depth and he regularly withheld information from the War Cabinet. Haig also secretly wrote to King George V and kept in touch with Lloyd George's predecessor, Herbert Asquith. Behind the scenes, Lloyd George did his best to remove Haig and, as we have seen, in 1917 managed to place him under the overall command of the Frenchman, Nivelle. In May 1918, Sir Frederick Maurice, a general at the War Office, accused the Prime Minister of deliberately withholding reserves from Haig to ensure that there would be no repeat of Passchendaele. In Parliament, Asquith pressed for an inquiry and the issue led to a motion of censure but Lloyd George survived. Haig detailed his own beliefs in a war of attrition when he said, 'The enemy should never be given a complete rest by day or by night, but be gradually and relentlessly worn down'. It was his view that the outcome of the war would be decided on the Western Front with victory going to the side that best withstood the rigours and losses required by trench warfare. However, Haig is not without admirers. In *Douglas Haig: The Educated Soldier* (1963), the historian John Terraine, makes a spirited defence of the field marshal and his tactics. Writing in *The Scotsman* in 1959, Major General Sir John Kennedy reminds us that 'His (Haig's) was the only army of the great nations at war that did not break'. Perhaps the most balanced consideration is that expressed by Gerard De Groot in *Douglas Haig 1861–1928* – 'It was Haig's fate that he, an eminent Edwardian, eventually came to be judged according to the very different standards of another age'.

The Italian Front

For the Italians, fighting was always going to be difficult in harsh Alpine terrain where the Austrians always held the higher slopes. General Luigi Cadorna commanded a sizeable army but it was badly trained, without battle experience and lacked modern weaponry, particularly artillery and transport. Cadorna, a competent general with an unfortunate personality, was arrogant, lacking in consideration for his ordinary soldiers and impatient with his subordinates and during the first 18 months of the war he dismissed 217 of his generals. The campaigns between the Italians and the Austro-Hungarians were fought in the foothills of the Alps close to the River Isonzo which rose in the mountains and reached the Adriatic Sea to the west of Trieste.

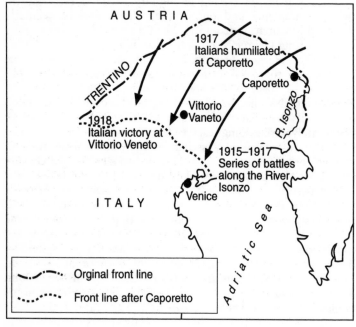

figure 21 the Italian Front 1915–17

The Battles of the Isonzo

Between 1915 and 1917, the conflict between the Italians and Austrians was almost totally limited to a series of battles fought along the River Isonzo. During 1915 alone there were four such battles and all of them ended inconclusively. Five more followed in 1916 and 1917 opened with the tenth and eleventh battles and in the last of these the Italians were sufficiently successful for the Austrians to ask for German help. The twelfth Battle of the Isonzo is better known as the Battle of Caporetto.

In what turned out to be the final battle fought along the River Isonzo, the Austrians backed by seven German divisions attacked the Italian positions. After a relatively brief bombardment, the Germans crossed the Isonzo, broke through the Italian lines and penetrated into the open ground beyond. As much of the routed Italian army turned and fled so the whole of the front line disintegrated and deserting soldiers heading for home blocked the roads and prevented the passage of vehicles carrying reserves and supplies to the war zone. The men had fought bravely enough but they had also suffered appallingly and their morale had been shattered. They no longer recognized a need to fight for king or country, they simply wanted to go home.

Cadorna had no choice other than to order a general retreat first to the River Tagliamento and then to the River Piave, in all a distance of some 95 kilometres (59 miles). With loyal Italian troops now holding good defensive positions and the enemy's supply lines overextended, the Austro-German advance came to an end. With 40,000 casualties and 300,000 soldiers taken prisoner, the Battle of Caporetto proved a major humiliation for Italy and led to a crisis that made it necessary for British and French divisions to be sent to reinforce their front. In its search for scapegoats, the Italian government blamed left-wing activists, defeatist attitudes and military incompetence and Cadorna was replaced by General Armando Diaz and a number of deserters were shot. However, the Caporetto fiasco did not mean that the Italian contribution to the war was over, far from it. It is interesting to note that one of the Italian soldiers serving at the front in the prestigious Bersaglieri Regiment was a 32-year-old sergeant, Benito Mussolini, who was destined to become the future Fascist dictator of Italy.

18 the collapse of Germany and the end of the war

This chapter will cover:
- the situation at the start of 1918
- America at war
- Ludendorff's final offensives
- the final collapse of Germany's allies
- Foch's final offensive
- the internal collapse of Germany and the threat of revolution.

'O Jesus, make it stop'.

(From *Attack* by Siegfried Sassoon, 1886–1967)

The overall situation at the start of 1918

With only the German submarine threat held at bay and victories in Palestine and Mesopotamia to set against major setbacks on the Western and Italian Fronts, 1917 was a bleak year for the Allies. The French army was still recovering from the disasters that led to open mutiny whilst, in spite of its heavy losses, the morale of the British army had taken a battering but was still largely intact. On both sides there were worrying manpower shortages and the new conscript armies did not always show the same fighting spirit as the legions that had fallen. For the Germans, the prospects were, if anything, even worse.

Germany in 1918

With the United States preparing to add her military and economic might to the Allied war effort, if Germany was going to win the war it was a case of now or never. The German High Command was faced with a race against time but there were also other reasons for concern. Whilst unrestricted submarine warfare had failed to starve Britain into submission, the Allied blockade of Germany was complete and on the home front the German people were suffering acute shortages. During the severe winter of 1916–17, food became so scarce that the Germans spoke of their 'turnip winter' and the situation worsened when, in 1917, the grain harvest was less than half that of 1913. Germany had also witnessed the first signs of popular unrest when during 1917 there were public demonstrations and protests and early in 1918, some 400,000 Berliners went on strike with the unrest soon spreading to other towns and cities across the country. The German parliament, the *Reichstag*, passed a resolution in favour of seeking a negotiated peace and within the traditionally moderate and largely popular German Social Democratic Party, an increasing number favoured a more positive anti-war line. The success of the Bolsheviks in Russia was also beginning to have an impact on German politics with the formation of a communist-backed Spartacist League. However, the German High Command dominated by Hindenburg and Ludendorff paid scant regard to

these events and Chancellor Bethmann Hollweg, who had
wanted to give peace proposals serious consideration, was
forced to resign.

America at war

Few Americans questioned Woodrow Wilson's decision to go to
war and, fuelled by stories of the 'Brutal Hun', there was an
immediate anti-German reaction. In some schools and colleges,
the teaching of German was dropped from the timetable,
German books disappeared from library shelves and even some
delicatessen stores renamed *sauerkraut* 'liberty cabbage'.
Although the United States had shipped supplies to the Allies, at
the time of her entry into the conflict she was strangely
unprepared for war. Whilst her army had no tanks and little
modern artillery and her air force had few aircraft suited to aerial
combat, her naval strength was considerable and several of her
battleships joined the British Grand Fleet at Scapa Flow. Her first
major task was to raise, train and equip an army for service in
Europe and this could not happen overnight. In order to make it
possible for America's industrial capacity to be converted to war
production, Congress granted the President near dictatorial
powers over much of the nation's economy and soon $44 million
per day was being poured into the nation's war effort.

The appearance of the first American troops in France, although
initially only a token force, provided a much needed boost to the
Allies. The American Commander-in-Chief, John Pershing, a
West Point graduate who had served in the American cavalry
during the Indian wars, had earlier suffered a personal loss
when his wife and three young children had perished in a fire.
Appointed to command the American Expeditionary Force in
1917, he was determined not to waste American lives in futile
trench warfare and held the view that his troops should not be
used in battle until he had 1 million under his command and
they could play a decisive role in the war. During the final stages
of the war, over 2 million American soldiers arrived in France
and as we shall see, they were to play an important role in the
defeat of Ludendorff's great offensives in 1918. They were to
suffer over 50,000 killed in battle.

In January 1918, Woodrow Wilson put forward his ideas for a
peace settlement. His proposals, known as his Fourteen Points,
set out to ban secret diplomacy, trade barriers and the mass
production of armaments that he considered the fundamental

causes of war, guarantee the freedom of the seas to all nations and offer all peoples self-determination, the right to decide their own destinies. He also wanted to establish a 'general association of nations' to regulate international affairs and ensure future world peace. However, confident that in the end victory would still be theirs, Germany rejected Wilson's ideas out of hand.

tactics. Surprise was to be all important to his new plan so that after a brief but intense bombardment of the Allied positions, small groups of elite shock troops or storm troopers would spearhead the attack, cut the wire and infiltrate the Allied lines. Once gaps had been made, the main force of German infantry would advance, exploit the gaps created, bypass strong points so that they could be dealt with later and then deploy into the open ground beyond. Since Pétain and Haig had different priorities, Allied defence strategy was unco-ordinated. Pétain was determined at all costs to prevent any German advance towards Paris whilst Haig recognized that it was essential for the British to protect the all-important Channel ports.

The first German offensive, 'Operation Michael' sometimes called *Kaiserschlacht* (the Kaiser's Battle), came in March 1918. Fought on the old Somme battlefields, on the opening day of the battle German shock troops, advancing behind a creeping barrage and smoke screen, used light machine guns and flame throwers to make breaches in the British lines. To the north, the British largely managed to hold their positions but to the south they were forced back towards Amiens. After ten days, the Germans had advanced 80 kilometres (50 miles) and were close to severing the link between the British and French positions. Even though reinforcements were rushed forward to plug the gap, the Germans advanced to within 100 kilometres (62 miles) of Paris so that their heavy guns were able to bombard the city. As the crisis deepened, the Supreme War Council met at Doullens and decided to appoint the Frenchman, Marshal Ferdinand Foch, to be commander-in-chief of all the Allied armies with Haig and Pétain as his subordinates. Under their new commander, the Allies rallied, halted and then reversed the German advance. Anyway, by this time exhaustion and problems caused by their now overextended supply lines had caused the German offensive to run out of steam. German soldiers had been told that Allied food shortages were as bad as their own but when they overran the British positions, they captured stores and supplies that proved this was not the case. The deceit adversely affected German morale and by the time Ludendorff called off 'Operation Michael', the Germans had sustained over 250,000 casualties and the British and French only 10,000 less. As the German commander ended one offensive, so he began another further to the north in Flanders.

The second German offensive, known as 'Operation Georgette', began in April to the south of Ypres just to the east of Armentières. With the British under enormous pressure, Haig issued an Order of the Day, 'There is no other course open to us but to fight it out! Every position must be held to the last man; there must be no retirement. With our backs to the wall and believing in the justice of our cause, each one of us must fight on to the end.' This time Ludendorff's aim was to sweep across Flanders and cut off the Channel ports of Boulogne, Calais and Dunkirk. The first German attack fell on a section of the line held by Portuguese troops (Germany had declared war on Portugal in 1916) where they gained some immediate success. The British also had to give up the ground gained at such enormous cost during the Passchendaele offensive the previous year. Fighting was particularly vicious around Mount Kemmel where land changed hands time and time again and by the end of the month the arrival of British reinforcements made Ludendorff call off his offensive. Again he had failed in his main objectives and the Channel ports remained secure in British hands. Losses were heavy on both sides – 76,000 British, 35,000 French, 6,000 Portuguese and 109,000 German. Even though his own troops were exhausted and demoralized and American troops were arriving in France in increasing numbers, Ludendorff was not finished and he now planned a new offensive along the River Aisne.

'Operation Blucher', the third and final German offensive, was against the French and started in May along a 40-kilometre (25-mile) front stretching from Soissons along the Chemin des Dames to Reims. The French were heavily outnumbered and this allowed the Germans to break through their lines, cross the River Aisne and advance towards the River Marne. The German advance was finally held by the French and Americans at Château Thierry and in mid-July, Foch unexpectedly ordered a massive counterattack that signalled the start of a German retreat. So Ludendorff's gamble had been in vain and with over 500,000 dead and wounded, his offensives had cost the German army dear. With barely any reserves left and supplies and munitions at an all time low, the morale of the German army finally disintegrated. On the other hand, with American troops arriving in France at a rate of 300,000 each month, Allied morale soared as they sensed that an end to the war might be in sight.

The collapse of Germany's allies

After years of relative inactivity, in September 1918 the Balkan Front came alive. From Salonika, British, French and Serbian forces moved against Germany's ally Bulgaria and with little prospect of receiving assistance, the Bulgarians were no match for the Allies. At the Battle of Vardar, the Serbs broke through the Bulgarian lines and afterwards their resistance along the whole front collapsed. In such a desperate situation, the Bulgarian government had no choice but to ask for peace and the war in the Balkans finally came to an end. The elimination of Bulgaria meant that additional Allied troops were available for use against the Turks.

You will remember that the situation on the Italian Front was delicate for both Italy and Austria alike. Now considered to be something of a liability by their Anglo-French allies, the Italians urgently needed to redeem their failures, particularly the disgrace of Caporetto, if they were to have any say in the post-war negotiations. In October 1918, the Italian armies under General Diaz and with the support of British and French units began operations aimed at gaining the initiative from the Austrians. Although they no longer had substantial German support, the Austrians resisted strongly but were nevertheless driven back from the River Piave towards the River Tagliomento where their whole front collapsed and they were forced to retreat in disorder until they stood to face the Italians at Vittorio Venito. Here the Italians won a resounding victory, took over 300,000 Austrian prisoners and avenged the humiliation of Caporetto. Afterwards the Austro-Hungarian government asked for peace and this was finally concluded on 4 November 1918.

Foch's final offensive

By August 1918, the initiative on the Western Front had passed to the Allies. With troop movements only made at night and secrecy so tight that even the divisional commanders were not aware what of was happening, the sudden Allied offensive took the Germans by surprise. With no preliminary barrage, British, French, Australian, and Canadian troops moved forward part hidden by mist and behind masses of light tanks. The Allies broke through the German lines with surprising ease and were able to capture objectives some ten kilometres (six miles) distant. Ludendorff later wrote, 'The 8th August was the black day of the German army in the history of the war ... Everything I had feared and of which I had so often given warning, had here, in one place, become a reality. Our war machine was no longer efficient.' The British again reached the old Somme battlefield where the momentum of their advance began to falter and faced by stiffening German resistance, Foch decided to switch his attack further to the north. By using a series of short but connected offensives, he was able to keep Allied casualties to a minimum and still force the enemy to retreat. Eventually the Germans found themselves back at the Hindenburg Line, the starting point of their first offensive five months earlier. On 12 September, the Americans attacked the German salient at St. Mihiel to the south-east of Verdun. In eliminating the salient, they took 15,000 prisoners but 7,000 of their own men were killed and wounded. A fortnight later, with the order '*Tout le monde à la batille*', 'Everyone to the battle', Foch began his final offensive against the Germans. To the south, the French and Americans attacked along the River Meuse and through the Argonne Forest whilst to the north, the British and Belgians made a renewed effort on the Ypres salient. As a pincer movement now threatened to encircle the Germans, they were forced to retreat further and with their fighting spirit broken, the Allies were able to break through the Hindenburg Line at several places with unexpected ease. In angry outbursts, Hindenburg blamed his failures on a lack of reserves, a shortage of munitions and the defeatist attitude of certain German politicians in the *Reichstag*. Faced with defeat on the battlefield and mounting unrest at home, Germany's military leaders realized that the need for an armistice was now an urgent necessity.

The final collapse of Germany

Not only were the German armies close to defeat but on the home front, the country was near to total economic collapse and in political turmoil. To add to their woes and in common with the rest of Europe and much of the world, Germany was in the grip of an influenza epidemic. Spanish influenza, so-called because one of the early victims was the King of Spain, was claiming more deaths than the battlefield and, short of medicines and with malnutrition rampant, on one day alone 1,700 Berliners died of the virus. On 29 September 1918, Ludendorff finally told the German government that the war was lost and that it was necessary to agree an armistice. The Allies refused to negotiate with Germany's military leaders and so Prince Max of Baden, a liberal with an international reputation for his work with the Red Cross, was appointed Chancellor and asked to form a government.

Recognizing that the terms outlined earlier in Wilson's Fourteen Points were likely to be more lenient than any offered by the Anglo-French allies, Prince Max used Swiss intermediaries to make contact with the American President. Woodrow Wilson's response was to first demand the withdrawal of German troops from all the territory they had occupied and he made it clear that the Allies would not negotiate with the Kaiser or the controlling military clique and insisted on the dismissal of the country's undemocratic rulers. Ludendorff was against acceptance and wanted to resume hostilities and make one last stand in order to save the honour of the German army. When this was rejected, both he and Hindenburg offered to resign but only his resignation was accepted. In haste, Ludendorff fled to Sweden in disguise. Prince Max now urged the Kaiser to abdicate but he refused stating, 'I would not dream of abandoning the throne because of a few hundred Jews and a thousand workers'. Consequently the situation took a turn for the worse.

Late in October, the German High Seas Fleet at Wilhelmshaven and Kiel was ordered to sea to engage the Royal Navy in a final act of defiance. The sailors, already demoralized by being confined to their home ports since 1915 and increasingly influenced by Bolshevik propaganda, mutinied. The disturbances spread quickly to other ports and workers' committees were set up in several towns and cities. Following demonstrations in Munich, a group of German Bolsheviks went as far as to declare Bavaria an independent socialist republic. With the situation getting out of hand, Prince Max advised Kaiser Wilhelm that if he persisted with his refusal to abdicate, he himself would resign. When revolutionaries took to the streets of Berlin and from the steps of the *Reichstag* building proclaimed a republic, Hindenburg warned the Kaiser that he could no longer guarantee his safety. So Wilhelm reluctantly abdicated, left Germany and sought political asylum in Holland.

The armistice signed

On 7 November, German delegates passed through the Allied lines, assembled in a railway carriage in a forest close to Compiègne and opened negotiations for an armistice. The French general Maxime Weygand recalled the occasion, '... a convoy of cars moving very fast appears on the road with no headlights on. On the front of the first one, a large white flag looms out of the darkness. A young officer identifies the bearers of the flag of truce and gets into the first of the five cars. The bugles sound another call whilst our soldiers look at the result of four years of fighting and suffering'.

The Allied representatives were Marshal Foch and General Weygand together with the British Admirals Hope and Wemyss whilst the German delegation of four was led by Mathias Erzberger who was later to be assassinated. The meeting was icy but correct with the armistice terms presented one by one and translated by an officer who read them in German. The German delegates were then given 72 hours to accept the terms on an understanding that a refusal would lead to the resumption of war. After days of frantic negotiations, the Germans finally signed the armistice at 5 a.m. on 11 November 1918. Word was then flashed to the world that the armistice would come into effect at 11 a.m. that same day.

And so the guns finally fell silent. In London, Paris and New York there were wild scenes as crowds celebrated in the streets; in Berlin there was an uneasy peace as the earlier disturbances still threatened to turn into a major uprising. In the House of Commons, Lloyd George said, 'I hope we may say thus, this fateful morning came to end all wars.'

The headlines of the *Evening Standard* on 11 November 1918.

19

the First World War – the cost

This chapter will cover:
- some retrospective views of the war
- the cost in human terms
- the cost in material terms
- the cost in financial terms
- other long-term consequences.

'If any question why we died,
Tell them because our fathers lied.'

(From *Common Form* by Rudyard Kipling, 1865–1936)

Some thoughts

The historian Peter Johnson has described the First World War as 'the greatest moral, spiritual and physical catastrophe in the history of the British people – a catastrophe whose consequences, all evil, are still with us' whilst Anthony Wood regards it as a time when 'the civilisation of the nineteenth century was blown to shreds' and 'a whole generation of young men were massacred in anonymous millions'. Sir Arthur Conan Doyle wrote, 'The system which left millions dead upon the fields of Europe must be rotten to the core … but one day the war may be regarded as the end of a dark age and the start of that upward path which leads away from personal and national selfishness.' Some war poets also recorded their thoughts:

They ask me where I've been,
And what I've done and seen.
But what can I reply
Who know it wasn't I,
But someone just like me,
Who went across the sea
And with my head and hands
Killed men in foreign lands …
Though I must bear the blame,
Because he bore my name.

(*Back* by Wilfred Gibson, 1878–1962)

Here dead we lie because we did not choose
To live and shame the land from which we sprung.
Life to be sure, is nothing much to lose;
But young men think it is, and we were young.

(*Here Dead We Lie* by A. E. Housman, 1859–1936)

Attempts have been made to calculate the human, material and financial costs of the First World War and express them as simple statistics but what figures can never take into account is the lasting impact of the death, destruction and dislocation of those years. It is impossible to place a money value on the suffering of those who lost limbs, returned blind or with minds damaged beyond recovery. One cannot measure the heartbreak and depth of grief of mothers and widows or the paternal affection never to be experienced by hosts of fatherless children. For each of those that did not return home, the so-called 'lost generation', there would be a grave or a name on a memorial but for the survivors of the trenches there would be memories and the struggle to settle once again to civilian life. British soldiers that returned home received the award of the War Medal and Victory Medal and for the families of those that died a bronze memorial plaque bearing the inscription 'died for freedom and honour'. Others were more fortunate. Field Marshal Haig was created an earl, received the thanks of Parliament and a grant of £100,000. French was made an earl whilst others such as Rawlinson, Gough, Hunter-Weston, Hamilton and Townshend were awarded knighthoods.

The balance sheet – the human cost

More than 68 million men were mobilized by the warring powers. Of these, an estimated 10 million died in battle and a further 21 million suffered wounds. It has been calculated that the average daily loss of life during the war was 5,509 whilst during the Boer War it had been just ten. The casualty rate of the Allies represented 52 per cent of the men mobilized; for the Central Powers it was 49 per cent.

Casualty figures – Allies and Central Powers

	Dead	Wounded	Missing
Allies	5,520,000	12,831,000	4,121,000
Central Powers	3,386,000	8,388,000	3,629,000

Casualty figures of the various warring nations

	Dead	Wounded
Germany	1,773,000	4,216,000
Russia	1,700,000	4,950,000
France	1,375,000	4,266,000
Austria-Hungary	1,200,000	3,620,000
Britain and the British Empire	1,013,000	2,090,000
Italy	650,000	947,000
Turkey	325,000	400,000
United States	126,000	234,000
Bulgaria	87,000	152,000
Serbia	45,000	133,000
Belgium	13,000	44,000
Portugal	7,000	13,000

In addition to the loss of life on the battlefields across Europe and the Middle East, an estimated 8.75 million civilians lost their lives. These were made up of those who died of disease and starvation, those who were victims of massacres and acts of genocide and those who died as a result of enemy action. To these must also be added the 8 million victims of the epidemic of Spanish influenza which occurred during the years 1918 and 1919.

The balance sheet – material cost

On the Western Front, the bulk of the fighting took place in Flanders and a region in north-east France between Verdun on the River Meuse across Picardie and Artois to the North Sea coast. In France alone, 2 million hectares (4.9 million acres) of agricultural land and 500,000 hectares (1.2 million acres) of forest were laid waste and some 3 million dwellings and buildings of all sorts destroyed. To this must be added the devastation wrought across Russia and Italy. In Britain, the damage caused by air raids and coastal bombardment was minimal. However, merchant-shipping losses were massive with 7.7 million tonnes, which exceeded those of the other Allies and Central Powers combined.

The balance sheet – financial cost

It has been estimated that the war cost over £75 billion. This sum was reached by adding together the expenditure of the governments involved, the capital value of human life – an estimate of what the men who lost their lives might have earned – the value of production lost due to the war and the repair costs of the buildings damaged. To this must be added the value of merchant shipping lost at sea, the losses suffered by neutral countries and the money spent on war relief. In order to finance the war, Britain borrowed £9.59 million, France £6.34 million and Italy £3.53 million all largely from the United States. The war over, these massive loans now had to be repaid. In Britain, the war saw rates of personal taxation increase from 9 per cent to 27 per cent whilst in France rates rose from 13 per cent to 18 per cent . German rates rose from 8 per cent to 12 per cent and in the United States from 2 per cent to 8 per cent . The gold reserves of all those involved in the war also fell substantially to the advantage of the United States and certain neutral countries.

The 'vast military holocaust' of the years 1914–18 saw the collapse of great empires and imperial dynasties – the Hohenzollerns in Germany, the Habsburgs in Austria-Hungary, the Romanovs in Russia and the sultans of the Ottoman Empire. Ordinary people would have to adjust to social, moral and cultural changes – their world would never be the same again.

A cartoon by an unknown British artist who used the pseudonym 'Caractacus'.
The cartoon bears the title 'The harvest of war is desolation and death'.

glossary

Allies Those countries that fought on the same side as Britain and France in the First World War.

amphibious operation A military operation in or on water.

annex To join or attach to.

bloc A combination of countries.

blockhouse A small fort.

camaraderie Good fellowship or comradeship.

Central Powers Those countries that fought on the same side as Germany in the First World War.

Colours A flag bearing the battle honours of a regiment.

compassionate leave Leave granted to a soldier facing personal or family problems.

constitution A system of laws according to which a country is run.

deadlock A situation in which matters have been brought to a standstill.

debauched Corrupt or over-indulged.

diplomatic manoeuvring Using diplomacy to gain an advantage.

esprit de corps Regard for the group or regiment to which one belongs.

estaminet A French café or bar.

fatigues Extra work or duties imposed on a soldier as a punishment.

flogging Lashing with a whip.

fraternized   To associate with or treat as brothers.

fuselage   The body of an aircraft.

Geneva Convention   An international agreement of 1864 regarding the treatment of wounded soldiers and prisoners of war.

howitzer   A large gun used in trench warfare.

impregnable   Impossible to capture or safe from attack.

inferiority complex   A feeling that one is of lesser quality to others.

irregular   A soldier not under official military authority.

jingoistic   Showing enthusiasm for war.

mobilize   To prepare armed services in readiness for war.

Pan Slav movement   A movement intended to bring all the Slav people together into one nation.

pincer movement   A manoeuvre intended to cut off or encircle the enemy.

posthumously   After death.

prima donna   Leading female singer or ballet dancer often considered to be very temperamental.

Pyrrhic victory   A victory gained at very great cost.

reconnaissance   A survey carried out to discover details of the enemy's position.

reservists   Part time soldiers liable to be called up at the time of an emergency.

respirators   Gas masks.

sniper   A skilled marksman who shoots at men from a distance.

subalterns   A junior army officer under the rank of captain.

stand to   The morning routine of men in the trenches. They stood to in expectation of an enemy attack since such attacks usually came in the morning.

ultimatum   A last offer or demand.

War Bonds   Stock (a type of share) sold by a government to help pay the costs of a war.

taking it further

Chapter 1

Further reading

The Archduke and the Assassin: Sarajevo June 28th 1914, Lavender Cassels (Dorset Press, 1984)

The Origins of the First World War, James Joll (Penguin, 1992)

The Great Naval Race: Anglo German Naval Rivalry, Peter Padfield (Hart-Davis, 1974)

War By Timetable, A. J. P. Taylor (American Heritage, 1969)

Guns in August, Barbara Tuchman (Ballentine Books, 1962)

Chapter 2

Further reading

The Vanished Army: The British Expeditionary Force 1914–15, Tim Carew (Kimber, 1964)

Death of an Army: The First Battle of Ypres, A. Farrar-Hockley (Arthur Barker, 1967)

The Opening Moves, John Keegan (Penguin, 1971)

The Schlieffen Plan, Gerhard Rutter (Wolff, 1958)

Mons John Terraine (Pan Books, 1960)

The Campaign on the Marne, Sewell Tyng (OUP, 1935)

Chapter 3

Further reading

The Great War in Africa, Byron Farwell (Viking, 1987)

German East Africa: The story of the First World War in East Africa, B. Gardner (Cassell, 1963)

Battle for the Bundu: The First World War in East Africa, Charles Miller (Macdonald & Jane, 1974)

Films

African Queen (1951) starring Humphrey Bogart and Katherine Hepburn is based on an episode in this campaign when, in 1915, a small riverboat is used to sink a German gunboat on Lake Tanganyika.

Chapter 4

Further reading

Tannenburg: The First Thirty Days in East Prussia, Edmund Ironside (Blackwood, 1925)

Carpathian Disaster: Death of an Army, Geoffrey Jules (Ballentine Books, 1970)

The Eastern Front 1914–17, Norman Stone (Hodder & Stoughton, 1975)

Chapter 5

Further reading

Gallipoli: One Long Grave, Kit Denton (Time/Life Books, 1986)

Damn the Dardanelles! The Agony of Gallipoli, John Laffin (Macmillan, 1985)

Gallipoli, Alan Moorhead (Hamish Hamilton, 1956)

Gallipoli, Robert Rhodes (Batsford, 1965)

Films

Apart from the BBC's *All the King's Men* (1999), other films covering the events of the Dardanelles campaign include the Australian made *Gallipoli* (1981) with Mark Lee, Mel Gibson and Bill Kerr and *ANZACS* (1985) starring Paul Hogan.

Chapter 6

195 taking it further

Further reading

The War the Infantry Knew, 1914–19, J. C. Dunn (Janes, 1987)

The Poor Bloody Infantry: The Truth Untold, W. H. A. Groom (Picardy, 1983)

The White Heat: The New Warfare, John Terraine (Sidgwick & Jackson, 1982)

Chapter 7

Further reading

Eye-Deep in Hell: Life in the Trenches, 1914–18, J. Ellis (Fontana, 1977)

The Face of Battle, John Keegan (Penguin, 1978)

The War in the Trenches, Alan Lloyd (Hart-Davis, 1987)

Films

All Quiet on the Western Front (1930) based on the book (1929) of the same name by the German Erich Maria Remarque is considered to be one of the finest anti-war films ever made. It was remade in 1979 starring Richard Thomas and Ernest Borgnine. *No Man's Land: Hell on Earth* (1931) is another account of life in the trenches as is the more recent *The Trench* (1999) starring Paul Nicholls and Daniel Craig.

Chapter 8

Further reading

British Gallantry Awards, P. E. Abbot and J. M. A. Tamplin (Guinness Superlatives, 1971)

The Monocled Mutineer, William Allison and John Fairley (Quartet Books, 1986)

For the Sake of Example, Anthony Babington (Leo Cooper, 1983)

Morale: A Study of Men and Courage, John Baynes (Leo Cooper, 1987)

Shot At Dawn, Julian Putkowski and Julian Sykes (Wharncliffe Publishing, 1989)

The Study of the Victoria Cross, Sir John Smythe (Muller, 1963)

Films

Paths of Glory (1957) starring Kirk Douglas, Adolphe Menjou and Wayne Morris tells the story of three Frenchmen court-martialled for cowardice. It is said that the trench scenes are amongst the most vivid ever made. The story of Percy Toplis is the subject of the much criticized BBC series *The Monocled Mutineer* with Paul McGann in the title role.

Chapter 9

Further reading

Verdun, Georges Blond (Andre Deutsch, 1965)

The *Battleground Europe* series (Leo Cooper) includes books that cover the various areas of the Somme battlefield

The Somme Then and Now, John Giles (After the Battle, 1986)

The Price of Glory: Verdun 1916, A. Home (Macmillan, 1972)

Somme, Lyn Macdonald (Michael Joseph, 1983)

The First Day of the Somme, Martin Middlebrook (Alan Lane, 1971)

Chapter 10

Further reading

Naval Battles of the First World War, Geoffrey Bennett (Batsford, 1968)

Jutland 1916, John Costello and Terry Hughes (Weidenfeld & Nicholson, 1976)

The Dreadnoughts, David Howarth (Time/Life Books, 1979)

The Great War At Sea, 1914–18, Richard Hough (Oxford University Press, 1983)

Chapter 11

Further reading

The Aeroplanes of the Royal Flying Corps, J. M. Bruce (Putman, 1962)

Aces High: The War in the Air Over the Western Front, A. Clark (Fontana, 1974)

The Great Air War, Aaron Norman (Macmillan, 1968)

Films

The first films made to illustrate the heroism and sacrifice of young airmen during the First World War were *The Dawn Patrol* (1930) which starred Douglas Fairbanks junior, and *Journey's End* (1930). The former was remade in 1938 with Errol Flynn in the central role; the latter, renamed *Aces High*, was remade in 1976 and starred Malcolm McDowell, Christopher Plummer and Simon Ward.

Chapter 12

Further reading

Fire Over England: The German Air Raids of World War I, H. G. Castle (Leo Cooper, 1982)

The Deluge: British Society and the First World War, Arthur Marwick (Bodley Head, 1965)

Great Britain and the War of 1914–18, I. Woodward (Methuen, 1967)

Chapter 13

Further reading

Secret Service, Christopher Andrew (Heinemann, 1985)

A History of the British Secret Service, Richard Deacon (Grafton Books, 1969)

Steinhauer: The Kaiser's Master Spy, Autobiography (John Lane, 1930)

The Secret Lives of Trebitsch Lincoln, Bernard Wasserstein (Penguin, 1988)

The Fatal Lover: Mata Hari, Julie Wheelwright (Collins & Brown, 1992)

Films

One of the most famous films made about espionage activities during the First World War was *The Thirty-Nine Steps* (1935) starring Robert Donat. The film was twice remade in 1959 and 1978 with Kenneth More and Robert Powell in the leading roles. Other films include *Mata Hari* (1931) with Greta Garbo in the title role and a remake in 1985 starring Sylvia Kristel. Conrad Veldt and Valerie Hobson appeared in *The Spy in Black* (1939), a melodrama about German spies operating in the Orkney Islands whilst *Zeppelin* (1971), with Michael York and

Marius Goring, tells of an attempt to steal secrets from the Zeppelin works at Friedrichshafen.

Chapter 14

Further reading

Some Corner of a Foreign Field: Poetry of the Great War, Ed. James Bentley (Little, Brown & Co, 1992)

Up the Line to Death: The War Poets 1914–18, Brian Gardner (Methuen, 1976)

The Best of Fragments From France, Bruce Bairnsfather, compiled by Tonie and Valmai Holt (Phin Publishing, 1978)

Poets of the First World War, Jon Stallworthy (Oxford University Press, 1974)

Chapter 15

Further reading

Ten Days That Shook the World, J. Reed (Boni & Liveright, 1919)

The Russian Army in World War I, Ward Rutherford (Gordon Cremonesi, 1975)

Quiet Flows the Don, Mikhail Sholokhov (recent edition Tuttle, 1996)

The Doughboys: The Story of the AEF 1917–18, Lawrence Stallings (Harper & Row, 1963)

The Zimmermann Telegram, Barbara Tuchman (Ballentine Books, 1958)

Films

The start of the films *Doctor Zhivago* (1965) starring Omar Sharif and Julie Christie and *Nicholas and Alexandra* (1971) provide accounts of events in Russia during the Revolutionary period.

Chapter 16

Further reading

Lawrence the Uncrowned King of Arabia, M. Asher (Penguin, 1999)

The Neglected War: Mesopotamia 1914–18, A. J. Baker (Faber, 1967)

Lawrence of Arabia, Robert Graves (Paragon, 1955)

Seven Pillars of Wisdom, T. E. Lawrence (Doran & Co, 1935)

Films

The most famous film about the campaign against the Turks in Palestine and Mesopotamia is David Lean's *Lawrence of Arabia* (1962) starring Peter O'Toole and Omar Sharif.

Chapter 17

Further reading

The Ironclads of Cambrai, Bryan Cooper (Souvenir Press, 1967)

They Called it Passchendaele: The Story of the Third Battle of Ypres, Lyn Macdonald (Michael Joseph, 1978)

Caporetto: The Scapegoat Battle, Ronald Seth (Macdonald, 1965)

Passchendaele, Philip Warner (Sidgwick & Jackson, 1987)

The First Tank Battle; Cambrai 1917, Robert Woolcombe (Arthur Baker, 1967)

Chapter 18

Further reading

The Kaiser's Battle, Martin Middlebrook (Allen Lane, 1978)

The Last Act, Barrie Pitt (Macmillan, 1962)

To Win a War: 1918 The Year of Victory, John Terraine (Sidgwick & Jackson, 1978)

No Man's Land: The Story of 1918, John Toland (Eyre & Methuen, 1980)

Films

Films about the involvement of the United States in the First World War include *Yankee Doodle Dandy* (1942) that tells the story of George H. Cohen with James Cagney in the title role and *Sergeant York* (1941) starring Gary Cooper and Walter Brennan.

Chapter 19

Further general reading

Testament of Youth, Vera Brittain (Gollancz, 1933)

World War I in Photographs, Adrian Gilbert (Orbis, 1986)

Goodbye to All That, Robert Graves (Penguin, 1973)

British Butchers and Bunglers of World War One, John Laffin (Sutton Publishing, 1989)

A Pictorial History of World War I, G. D. Sheffield (Bison Books, 1987)

Memoirs of an Infantry Officer, Siegfried Sassoon (Faber & Faber, 1930)

Lions Led By Donkeys, P. A. Thompson (Warner Laurie, 1927)

Mr Punch's History of the Great War, (Cassell & Co, 1919)

index

teach yourself **history**

a completely new series in the **teach yourself** range

the cold war
0340 884940 £8.99

nazi germany
0340 884908 £8.99

the middle east
0340 884916 £8.99

the second world war
0340 884932 £8.99

special forces
0340 884924 £8.99

the first world war
0340 884894 £8.99

teach yourself

the second world war
alan farmer

- Explore the events of the Second World War
- Discover its impact on those involved
- Understand the reasons behind the conflict and who was to blame

teach yourself the second world war is an accessible introduction to one of the most important, tragic and costly events in history. This war had an unimaginable impact on the entire world, causing the deaths of over 50 million people. Follow the main military campaigns of the war, discover how it affected the countries involved and develop your understanding of why the Allied powers were able to achieve victory.

Alan Farmer is Head of History at St Martin's College, Lancaster and has written a large number of books on modern American, European and British history.

teach
yourself

the middle east since 1945
stewart ross

- Read an accessible guide to today's political hotspot
- Understand the development of the region
- Discover more about a major world issue

teach yourself the middle east since 1945 tells the story of the modern world's most troubled region. It is lively yet authoritative, examining the origin and developments of issues that have made the headlines over the last half century. This book addresses many questions about the region, including why the Israeli–Palestinian conflict has lasted so long and the background to the two Gulf Wars and presents each aspect with engaging objectivity.

Stewart Ross taught in a variety of institutions worldwide before becoming a writer, lecturer and broadcaster. He has written over 175 books, including widely acclaimed historical works.

nazi germany
michael lynch

- Discover this extraordinary period
- Understand the motives of the individuals who created and led the Nazi movement
- Gain an insight into the experiences of those involved

teach yourself nazi germany is an accessible introduction to one of the most controversial periods in modern history. The years 1933–45 witnessed the take-over of Germany by a man and a movement whose racial and political policies are now regarded with universal abhorrence. Yet in all of European history there has never been a more genuinely popular regime than that of the Nazis. This book immerses you in the remarkable Third Reich story and the controversies that still surround it.

Michael Lynch is a tutor at the University of Leicester and is also a writer, specializing in modern European and Asian history.

the cold war
c. b. jones

- Understand the period that gave us the Cuban crisis, the Berlin wall, nuclear weapons and James Bond
- Discover more about this hidden conflict
- Read a compelling guide to this 45-year-long war

teach yourself the cold war is an accessible introduction to a war that shaped the latter half of the twentieth century. It covers all aspects, from questioning whether the tension really ended with the fall of the Berlin wall, to examining what JFK and his assassin had in common. Understand the global reach of this hidden conflict and its effects on the world in recent history and today.

C. B. Jones is an experienced teacher and Head of Faculty. She is also an A Level examiner with a specialist knowledge of twentieth century history.

teach yourself | **special forces**
anthony kemp

- Gain an overview of the history of Special Forces
- Understand how anti-terrorist units function
- Find out how Special Forces began and evolved

teach yourself special forces is a concise introduction to the secret world of Special Forces units, giving you a fascinating insight into how they are recruited, trained and armed, what they can and cannot achieve, and their role in controlling modern-day terrorism. Read a compelling history of Special Forces, from the birth of small-scale raiding forces during the Second World War, to the Iranian Embassy siege.

Anthony Kemp is an established military historian, writer and film producer who specializes in the Special Air Service Regiment.

teach yourself ®

Afrikaans
Access 2002
Accounting, Basic
Alexander Technique
Algebra
Arabic
Arabic Script, Beginner's
Aromatherapy
Astronomy
Bach Flower Remedies
Bengali
Better Chess
Better Handwriting
Biology
Body Language
Book Keeping
Book Keeping & Accounting
Brazilian Portuguese
Bridge
Buddhism
Buddhism, 101 Key Ideas
Bulgarian
Business Studies
Business Studies, 101 Key Ideas
C++
Calculus
Calligraphy
Cantonese
Card Games
Catalan
Chemistry, 101 Key Ideas
Chess
Chi Kung
Chinese
Chinese, Beginner's

Chinese Script, Beginner's
Christianity
Classical Music
Copywriting
Counselling
Creative Writing
Crime Fiction
Croatian
Crystal Healing
Czech
Danish
Desktop Publishing
Digital Photography
Digital Video & PC Editing
Drawing
Dream Interpretation
Dutch
Dutch, Beginner's
Dutch Dictionary
Dutch Grammar
Eastern Philosophy
ECDL
E-Commerce
Economics, 101 Key Ideas
Electronics
English, American (EFL)
English as a Foreign Language
English, Correct
English Grammar
English Grammar (EFL)
English for International Business
English Vocabulary
Ethics
Excel 2002
Feng Shui

Film Making
Film Studies
Finance for non-Financial Managers
Finnish
Flexible Working
Flower Arranging
French
French, Beginner's
French Grammar
French Grammar, Quick Fix
French, Instant
French, Improve your
French Starter Kit
French Verbs
French Vocabulary
Gaelic
Gaelic Dictionary
Gardening
Genetics
Geology
German
German, Beginner's
German Grammar
German Grammar, Quick Fix
German, Instant
German, Improve your
German Verbs
German Vocabulary
Go
Golf
Greek
Greek, Ancient
Greek, Beginner's
Greek, Instant
Greek, New Testament
Greek Script, Beginner's
Guitar
Gulf Arabic
Hand Reflexology
Hebrew, Biblical
Herbal Medicine
Hieroglyphics
Hindi
Hindi, Beginner's
Hindi Script, Beginner's
Hinduism
History, 101 Key Ideas
How to Win at Horse Racing
How to Win at Poker
HTML Publishing on the WWW
Human Anatomy & Physiology
Hungarian
Icelandic
Indian Head Massage

available from bookshops and on-line retailers